SAVE IT,
INVEST IT,
AND RETIRE

SAVE IT,
INVEST IT,
AND RETIRE

by DONALD I. ROGERS

ARLINGTON HOUSE   *New Rochelle, N.Y.*

Library of Congress Catalog Card Number 72-91634

ISBN 0-87000-202-3

MANUFACTURED IN THE UNITED STATES OF AMERICA

This book
is dedicated to the memory of
Eva Driggs Rogers and Ernest E. Rogers

Foreword

DON ROGERS IS A MAN WHO WRITES BOOKS PEOPLE NEED.

His *Teach Your Wife to Be a Widow* was much needed and is the only book I know of its kind.

Mr. Rogers was financial editor of the New York *Herald Tribune* and knows whereof he speaks. *Save It, Invest It, and Retire* is another book people need and one from which they can benefit.

Mr. Rogers has written a book that is as timely as today. It is written about today's problems for today's people in today's economic environment. Outmoded investment precepts are completely discarded.

He also stands revealed as a very human person with an understanding of and concern for not only the problems of the individual but also of the society in which we live.

He will start you thinking about why you are working. Today he says it is more of a problem of what to do with one's rewards than to find employment. He knows we have learned to sow but not to reap. His book will help readers along the way.

He knows, too, that it is as difficult for the 150,000-dollar-a-year man as the copy boy to save—he will suggest how much —and how to succeed at it. Some of his dissertations that kindled my thinking were:

The Difference Between A Saver and A Hoarder
Don't Save for A Rainy Day
When Houses Are Not Investments
Banks Think the Opposite of Investors
The Four-Plus Costs of Home Ownership
Investing in Stocks Is Not As Risky As Many People Say
The Way to Success Is Through Speculation
Don't Retire Until You Are Ready on Two Counts
Cashing in on Life Insurance at Retirement
Life's Fourth Phase

The reader will find everything he needs in this book to know about saving in real estate through home ownership, through insurance, and in fact the total ground rules of personal budgets.

Next, he will be told about making money in the stock market and about that important day when what he invests from his dividends exceeds what is invested from savings. Mutual funds, monthly investment plans, dollar averaging, even tax exempts, are discussed—the coverage is complete.

Finally, all about retirement—when—the key to doing it successfully—financing retirement—things to do after retirement.

The book closes with a glossary of stock market terms, and included are charts, tables and lists that are most helpful.

I would be less than human if I did not mention that Mr. Rogers finds Wall Street financiers about the nicest folks one can meet—which is just what I found in 1923 when I came from San Francisco to what I was warned was a cold, heartless, and calculating environment. Like Mr. Rogers, I met the nicest folks I ever knew, Don Rogers among them. This is a book written for the 17,000,000 American families who have saved 1000 dollars or more and have yet to learn about investing. It is also a book for the estimated 6,500,000 Americans who now own common stock. But above all, it is a book for all of us who don't save as much as we would like and want to learn how— who are confused about the merits and demerits of home ownership—who have yet to learn how life insurance can be living insurance—and above all—who are so occupied in providing what we think are the necessities of our everyday life that we fail to stop and plan to collect the rewards.

G. M. LOEB.

Preface: The Nicest Folks You Can Meet

I WAS VASTLY AMUSED WHEN I FIRST SAW CLARENCE DAY'S PLAY, *Life with Father,* for Father Day was prone to read his old New York *Tribune* over the breakfast coffee and explode about "that damned New Haven Railroad." Though my childhood followed by many years the one described by Mr. Day, my earliest recollections are of my father, reading his New York *Herald Tribune* and shouting virtually the same indictment about the same railroad. At times he broadened it to cover the Central New England Railroad which ran on the west side of the Farmington River in my home town of New Hartford, Connecticut, while the New York, New Haven & Hartford ran up the east side.

Apparently a great many businessmen in New York and New England had spent a great deal of money for the securities of their "local" railroads.

The point is, I got a bad early impression of the corporate giant known as the New Haven Railroad which friendship in later years with three succeeding presidents of the line has never succeeded in quite dispelling.

At the most impressionable point in my adolescence the nation and the world were plunged into history's worst depression and for years, wherever and whenever I overheard older and wiser men discussing finances or economics, I heard heated abuse of "that Wall Street crowd."

Later, when World War II came along and I was picked by my friends and neighbors to represent them in the draft, I met a great many soldiers who spoke bitterly about the "warmongers" of Wall Street. I know now that this was propaganda, planted by a clever foe and peddled by the ignorant among us.

In school I learned about the evils of Wall Street financiers in past generations; I learned little, if anything, about today's

Wall Streeters. I learned in school that Big Business is bad and I was made to feel that the poor people were on the side of right as opposed to the side of might.

Like most Americans I was taught to confuse poverty with meekness, and I was taught that meekness is a virtue, for does it not say in the Beatitudes that the meek are blessed, and that they will inherit the earth?

Long before I came to Wall Street, however, I had discovered that all of my beliefs about capitalists, brokers, financiers, and traders were completely wrong. I learned that some of the hardest-working, most sincere, most patriotic, and most honorable men work in Wall Street.

Since becoming part of the financial community on Manhattan's tip I have learned something else: that these folks, these financiers, are some of the finest people you can meet—anywhere.

I salute them, and I hail their work and what it means to our nation and to our individual freedom. I salute the Wall Streeters who stood steadfast during one of the most vicious and wicked propaganda campaigns in history and who recognized long before many of us that the *only* assurance of individual freedom can come from a system of free enterprise, and who have never been ashamed to call it by its right name—capitalism. For we are only as free as our jobs are free.

I salute them, and I thank them.

Despite their enormously heavy work schedules and their back-breaking responsibilities, a great many of them took time off to help me in the preparation of this book. Therefore the author wishes to express herewith his grateful appreciation to the following men who, one and all, are proud to be called "Wall Streeters":

Mr. G. Keith Funston, president, New York Stock Exchange; Mr. Cecil MacCoy, vice-president, New York Stock Exchange; Mr. Edward T. McCormick, president, American Stock Exchange; Mr. John Sheehan, director of public relations and advertising, American Stock Exchange; Mr. Winthrop H. Smith, managing partner, Merrill Lynch, Pierce, Fenner & Beane; Mr. Gerald M. Loeb, a senior partner, E. F. Hutton & Company; Mr. Robert W. Purcell, chairman of the board, Investors Diversified Services, Inc.; Mr. Walter L. Morgan, president, The Wellington Company; Mr. Perry Hall, senior partner, Morgan Stanley & Co.; Mr. Harold Bache, senior partner, Bache & Company; Mr. Chapin S. Newhard, senior partner, Newhard, Cook & Co.; Mr. Thomas F. Staley, senior partner, Reynolds & Co.; Mr. Carl Cefola, director of public information, The Mutual Life Insurance Company of New York; and, of course, my secretary, Mrs. Gertrude E. Finn, whose indispensable assistance is beyond value or calculation.

D. I. R.

.... And Some After Thoughts:
Some of the folks listed in the foregoing have left the Wall Street scene either for other careers or for the Ultimate Reward —among the latter, my friend and secretary, Mrs. Finn, and, of course, the *Herald Tribune* has gone, too. It impresses me, though, that after nearly twenty years, Wall Street remains so unchanged and, well, unchangeable.

I have felt obliged to make several "updating" revisions in the manuscript for this book, but not as many as I had imagined would be needed. There are more people investing in the stock market today, over 35 million of them, but I am not sure that general comprehension of the capitalistic system is any greater today than it was in 1955 when I wrote the original manuscript. It is in Wall Street that the verities of the system are observed without question: that capital formation buys the tools of production; that the tools of production create earnings and profits; that earnings and profits create jobs; that jobs create consumers to use the products made by the tools; and that the source of it all is capital formation, which is the *raison d'etre* of Wall Street. It is still America's main artery, perhaps the world's.

D.I.R.

Ridgefield, Conn.
1972

Contents

Introduction: Why Are *You* Working?

HARDLY AN ENGLISH-SPEAKING CHILD HAS NOT, DURING THE COURSE of his school, sat in some auditorium and listened to the stirring, challenging declaration of William Ernest Henley's *"Invictus,"* "I am the master of my fate; I am the captain of my soul." On most adolescent ears the inspiration is wasted, the admonishment unneeded and unnoticed, for a child is his own master, his soul well-commanded, his destination pursued with valorous vector.

What pity that Henley's simple words are not more eminent in adult culture. There are few masters or captains among the mature. Most adults are not Ablebodied Seamen on their individual ships; they do not chart the course or fix their position on life's seas.

Why work: Why struggle? What do we seek? What is our gain, our aim, our destination?

We have molded an incomparable way of life with the argil of industriousness leavened with compassion; we call it free enterprise, and for it we shed blood and sacrifice sons and consecrate wealth and possessions.

Have we secured the freedom of enterprise at the cost of individual independence? In our desire for a snug, safe, well-commanded ship have we surrendered our right to a voice in the decision on its destination? Enlarging Henley's theme, have we forsaken the command of our own small boats for the irresponsible security of crewmen on the large ship?

Few work for pleasure, for dedication; most for gain. What price the gain? What *use* the gain?

Employment is not the problem of Atomic Age man; there is remunerative work aplenty. We have taught man how to work; we have not taught him what to do with his labor's rewards. We have learned how to sow, not how to reap.

We tax our earnings as we tax our independence of decision,

and in so doing we regiment our futures as we regiment our workdays. Atomic Age man will find it difficult to earn enough wealth to buy his own freedom. Will we work until we drop in old age, or shall we as so many do, join with fellow workers to persuade our employers and our legislators to insure our security in our late years of life?

Or shall we adjust to our times and our way of life, learn how to save, learn how to invest, and assume command of our lives so that we may each chart our individual courses to the destinations of our choice—to proud, self-accomplished independence in the harvest years when we have earned the right to retire?

DONALD I. ROGERS.

New York City
January, 1956

. . . . After Nearly Two Decades. . . .

Have we learned, have we profited from past experience? Now, more than ever, one can ask: "What ever happened to the spirit of 'Invictus?' " Now, more than ever, it is necessary to learn how to chart one's own course and how to pilot oneself along it to a self-selected destination.

The choices remain with us.

DONALD I. ROGERS

Ridgefield, Connecticut
1972

Part I

Save It

Chapter 1

Savings from Income

I HAVE NEVER LIKED TO SAVE MONEY. THE VIRTUE OF THRIFT HAS never been mine rightfully to enjoy or espouse. It took me nearly thirty-five years to learn that the coiners of those hard-minted Yankee adages like *"A Penny Saved Is A Penny Earned"* were peddling sound advice.

It has been a psychological problem. A depression-dominated boyhood and fretful adolescence in a small Connecticut town created in me a deep-seated dislike of anything that hinted at thrift. It required major mental effort for me to recognize, in time to avoid a wastrel's existence, that there's an immense difference between those two overworked words of the apprehensive hoarders of money, "prudence" and "parismony."

It took so long to shake off the unwholesome influence of a pitiful, dour Scotch great-aunt of mine, a post-middle-aged widow who faced a bleak future on dwindling resources, that it is unlikely I ever would have embraced prudent thrift as an integral part of a well-planned life had not the responsibilities of a family of my own caused me to give it some thought.

Indeed, as a student of business and economics, I have written thousands of words on the necessity of Americans to spend —and keep spending—if we are to keep industry's wheels turning and the employment rolls comfortably filled. For the constant circulation of money is the outstanding basic feature of the American economic system.

But there are two kinds of savers, the "optimistic savers" and the "apprehensive savers."

Those who save optimistically save so they'll be free of total dependence on a current income. They save for college educations for the children. They save for ultimate retirement and a life of ease. They save for a possible period of unemployment or a siege of sickness. They save so they can buy a car or a home or a kitchen appliance. They save so they'll have money handy in the event an opportune investment happens along.

Those who save apprehensively save for "a rainy day," a phrase which to my mind is one of the meanest and unhappiest expressions in our domestic lexicon. These apprehensive savers aren't savers at all, but hoarders—misers, in degree—who live in fear of old age, sickness, or unemployment. They extract their money from the economy and spend what they must gloomily and grudgingly. Their psychological problem is far more severe, more retarding to our nation's economic health, than the one which afflicted me before I sighted "balanced thrift" in its proper perspective.

Thus, although I am presenting a book which deals in part with thrift, I am advocating only "balanced thrift," a vague term, I'll admit, but one which I'll try to explain.

For most, there's only one source for savings, and that's from a weekly or monthly income paid in the form of wages or salary for services performed. It's not easy to take from this income any part, no matter how small, for savings.

I count among my friends many in varied income levels, whose incomes range from the few weekly dollars of my own copy boy to the thousands of dollars a week of the presidents of the nation's largest corporations. It seems unbelievable, but it is as hard for the $250,000-a-year man to save any money as it is for the copy boy who is paying college tuition from his comparatively meager salary.

Thus it's a remarkable fact that when anyone thinks of thrift or savings, he does so guiltily and with many self-accusations. After polling a great many people I have concluded that not one feels he is saving enough of his money, saving wisely, or gaining sufficient security through his savings program.

The big question is: *How Much Should One Save from His Pay?*

It's a remarkable American characteristic that everyone lives up to his income. It makes little difference how much a person earns—he'll spend it all, or most of it. The savings ratio of the knights of industry and the princes of Wall Street is not, as a rule, much greater than that of the white-collar workers in their employ, and it's generally on a par with or even less than the savings ratio of the industrial workers with peak skills (which gives them premium pay) and small families (which make only moderate demands on the income).

The mere fact that the seemingly privileged own yachts or take glamorous winter vacations means only that they're spending more from income or have favorable tax positions. It doesn't mean that they're saving more of their money or that their old ages have, perforce, become more secure.

Though bankers guard carefully the confidences of their customers, I have checked a large number of them and find they'll admit to this much: that generally the biggest savings accounts do not belong to their wealthiest customers. Or, put another way, the customers with the highest incomes are not the ones who save the most money.

It's fortunate for America that this is one of our national traits. The fact that we spend most of what we earn has been the greatest single force behind our fantastic industrial growth. If we saved it all, we'd have turned out to be a capitalistic nation in the sense that Britain's cautious investors are capitalistic, instead of a management-run industrial nation.

How much to save is a hard thing to determine. There's no real guide, no definite code.

I put my own calculations in percentages, but it should be remembered that I'm talking of incomes based on the purchasing power of the dollar and the tax laws of 1972 and that, irrevocably, things will change.

Another thing, the use of that term, "A Family of Four," has always confused me for I never knew whether they were referring to a man, wife, and two children, or a couple with four children, so to make this clear, I'll state definitely that the following calculations are based on a family consisting of four persons: a man, his wife, and two children.

If Your Weekly Income Is:	You Should Save Approximately:
$65—$75	3%
$75—$95	4%
$95—$140	5%
$140—$195	6%—8%
$195—$225	8%—9%
$225—$500	10%
$500—$800	6%—8%
$800 or more	10% or more

You will note that I have suggested that a person earning $500 to $800 a week save a smaller percentage of his income than a person earning $225 to $500 a week. The reason for that is apparent to one who studies the existing tax laws. There's another factor of equal importance. It's the "keeping up with the Joneses" concept of America's social life, a difficult-to-ignore condition that hits with severe impact in that income bracket, much more so than in the next-lower and next-higher brackets.

In most commerical and professional endeavors the man earning $500 to $800 a week cannot permit himself the pleasures of the quiet, retiring life. Indeed, in most communities and in most business situations that yield him that kind of money, he's bound by the conventions and mores to be a significant social goliath.

The savings of Americans—the wonderful habit of thrift—has become an important part of the nation's economy, important in planning both by government and business. It will increase in importance as time goes on.

There's a good reason for this.

Until a few years ago, the distribution of the nation's wealth was like a pyramid:

There were a very few rich people at the top, and a very large number of poor people at the bottom.

But today that has changed. The pyramid has become a diamond, or two pyramids, like this:

There are still a very few rich people at the top. But there are only a few poor people at the bottom. The wealth is distributed among the great number of Americans in the middle.

In a changing world with changing economies this has been accomplished without too many painful dislocations. It is a superior result to that in England, where the once-similar pyramid has been changed to appear like this:

In other words, no more rich people in England.

Shortly before the first edition of this book was written,

America had experienced its first genuine postwar "recession." Yet, despite the decline in production and employment, personal savings of Americans continued to grow.

Why was this, when all the econc.nists viewing their statistics and charts advised us that we were "tapering off"?

Actually it wasn't surprising, since income remained at a high level while spending declined. Total national income was reduced. But those who continued at their jobs earned just about as much as they had before. Rather than spend it, they saved it.

During the early days of the war in Vietnam we heard a great deal about "scare buying" when people besieged the stores and shops with their open wallets, anxious to buy almost anything at all on the theory that the price would rise prohibitively or that things would become unavailable. In times to come, when the twentieth century's economic history is written, that period will probably be known as the time of "scare saving."

People saved for two reasons: *1.* They feared another depression liked the one of 1929–38; and *2.* They expected prices to be reduced, hence they expected to enjoy some kind of "inventory appreciation" on their saved dollars. Neither of these conditions came about.

This is not the type of saving I advocate. In America, with her peculiar and particular type of economy, this is, in fact, destructive saving. It cuts off the fuel from the economic machine and the whole business slows down. For America is a mighty, complex machine, powered by dollars and lubricated by sweat. Take away the power and the whole contraption slows and much of the hard-bought lubrication is wasted.

When most economists or government experts discuss savings, they seem to assume that most Americans either work for someone at a salary or own farms. Omitted from the calculations and advices are those millions who are self-employed and who own their own businesses.

How do these "independents" save their money systematically?

The first great accomplishment, with the self-employed as well as with the wage earner or salaried individual, is to recognize at the outset that no great amount of saving will ever be accomplished until saving becomes an *obligation*.

It has to be a *regular charge against income,* just like rent or taxes or the light bill. And it has to be paid regularly, with proper recognition of delinquencies.

If you skip a month, you *owe* that month's savings to yourself —and make sure you dun yourself until you get it!

The greatest problem cases among the self-employed are the professional men; the doctors, dentists, and lawyers. They're too busy in their dedicated tasks to take care of their personal finances. From the telephone calls and letters I get asking for counsel, I'd judge that the men of medicine are probably the most duped or misled educated individuals in the whole field of personal finance. Many of them hardly know what they're about when it comes to saving their money or investing it. They're too busy—put in too many hours saving lives—to give much thought to saving money.

By most standards they're just about the ripest "suckers" around. A majority of them earn good incomes. Few of them have the time or information necessary to handle their money once they've earned it.

As a result they've probably been hooked into more unworthy schemes than any single class of people.

One of my first assignments on the old New York *Herald Tribune* was the creation of a weekly column rounding up the business-financial-economic news of the preceding seven days. It is a principal concept of journalism as it was practiced at the *Herald Tribune* that most Americans have become far too busy on weekdays to want to be "educated" when they read their morning papers—that they prefer to be informed, completely, though rapidly and entertainingly.

It soon became apparent to me that there was, perhaps, one group of citizens who were too busy even to be gently informed on news events *each* weekday and that in the course of a week there were a couple of days when they didn't get a chance to see any newspaper. I mean, of course, doctors.

Hardly had the column started when I was bombarded with letters of inquiry from the doctors and dentists. They wanted to know more about various items I had summarized on the preceding Sunday. One busy medic explained this delightful rash of fan mail with a plaintive appeal for counsel:

> I assume there are many other general practitioners who are in my predicament [he said]. I have been building my practice for fifteen years and it's a pretty good one. I have a good income from it and can live well, or at least my family can. I can manage to save an interesting amount of money each year.
>
> But what do I do with it after I save it? I don't think I should leave all of it in savings accounts.
>
> Yet I'm much too busy to pay any attention to the stock market or to give any thought to investments. If I do any reading at all, I can't waste my time reading up about the economy of certain industries or particular corporations. I have to catch up on what has been happening in my own profession. Doctoring takes all my time. That's why this weekly summary of yours helps.

Here's one situation, certainly, which proves that the old adage about "them as has, gits," is not always applicable.

The owners of small businesses often voice the same complaint; they're too busy to think about their savings program or about any investment other than the one they have made in time and money in their own business. Like the doctors, they live with a single purpose to the exclusion of personal considerations.

At this point we're thinking only of savings, not yet of investments.

Moreover, we're thinking only of cash savings, not of savings in real estate, insurance, or increment in businesses.

How do these independent businessmen and professional men accumulate their cash savings? It's ridiculously simple, but very few of them do it.

They must do the same as the wage and salary earners do—save systematically and make regular *charges* against income.

Every doctor knows that he has to pay his light bill. He has to pay his rent or mortgage. He has to buy a new car every other year or so, hence makes a charge against his income to provide for it.

Every businessman knows he has to have these same charges—light, heat, rent, all those things that go to comprise that monstrously overstuffed accounting term, "overhead."

There's no reason why savings can't become an irrevocable part of overhead.

But it should be calculated on an annual basis and paid off weekly or monthly.

In these days of income taxes, everyone is required to know his annual income and to make computations from it. Assume that a businessman knows that his annual net income, before taxes, will be $15,000. That's a little more than $288 a week.

Looking back to the table on page 24, he'd find that the recommended saving for anyone earning between $225 and $500 a week is 10 per cent.

So $28 weekly is saved. Or it can be $112 monthly, if it's easier to handle that way.

But it should be a regular charge—an irrevocable and unavoidable charge—one which, if it falls behind for a month, becomes due and payable.

It is easy for anyone to sit smugly and comfortably behind his own savings program and tell someone else how to do it. Perhaps the percentages recommended on page 24 cannot apply in particular cases. Perhaps there are certain drains on personal income, like unwieldy debts, that prohibit such a rate of saving. However, generally speaking, this much saving should be attainable. Put it this way: it should be attainable if you want to build the kind of program that will permit you to invest competently and ultimately to retire.

A large number of businessmen pay themselves straight salaries out of their businesses. Perhaps these are the best managers and theirs are the best-run businesses.

They will have to figure out their own savings ratios. Perhaps the savings rate should be applied to the salary they pay themselves, or perhaps it should be applied to the total net profit, before taxes, at the end of the year. It depends on what happens to the money left over after the salary is paid. If the money reverts to the owner, then it's income and the tax for savings should be made against it. If it is put back into the business for expansion or improvement, it shouldn't be regarded as subject to the charge for savings, since it's already working for the owner as invested capital.

But the trick with savings—with a savings program—is to make it specific, to make it systematic, to make it unrelenting and constant.

If the businessman netting his $288 a week cannot save $28 a week because of individual circumstances, but finds, after thoughtful analysis, that he can afford $18 a week, then he should save $18 a week come hell or high water.

The same holds true for the salaried man or wage earner. Fix your percentage, then stick to it.

But suppose a bad week comes along. Little Johnny's tonsils have to come out. The furnace breaks down. The picture tube on the TV set blows out. And this is the week your Missus has to have that new formal in Saks Fifth Avenue window, because she's accompanying you to that convention next week.

What a week! If there ever was a week when you should be entitled to skip that charge for savings, this is the one!

Don't kid yourself. This is the very week you need savings the most. Make that savings a tax against your income, just as though it were the smoothest, easiest week you'd ever had. Because, as you can see, you're going to need that money.

Just calm down. Think about it. Your budget is set up to handle new clothes. You're required by law to keep your wife attired. You had anticipated this expense. She's probably going to charge it anyway. Your salary isn't going to get belted with that cost this week.

Sure, you say, but what about Johnny and the furnace and the TV tube?

All right, but make this a calm appraisal. This is an emergency, so keep a level head. Take smallest things first. That TV picture tube. Why, that's only $125.00, plus a $20.00 installation charge. Certainly your family budget is flexible enough to handle that? You have *that* much elasticity in your checking account, haven't you?

Johnny's tonsils are going to cost $300. The furnace, the repair man told you, is going to cost $225.50. So you need $670.50 in cash to make this terrible week into a tolerable week.

That's precisely what you've been saving your money for. While you're at the bank depositing this week's savings, make out a withdrawal slip for $670.50, transfer it to your checking account, and your problems are solved. Just make sure you deposit this week's savings though.

Easy, isn't it? Just keep in mind that you're not hoarding money—you're saving it. You saved it, among other things, for just such an emergency.

You don't have to feel that your savings account is $670.50 in the red—or is minus $670.50—because of the withdrawal you made. Forget the balance, disregard the total of the account. Just keep making the regular savings payment to the account. The only time you need to be concerned is when you are delinquent in your payments.

This is the difference between the hoarder and the saver. The hoarder saves every penny he can. He begrudges every penny he spends. He accumulates as much in savings as he possibly can and is frantic when he has to dip into them for such emergencies as a tonsillectomy or a broken furnace. He hasn't a savings "program." He has a way of life.

The person who has a schedule for savings is not a hoarder. He saves because it's necessary to a well-planned life and an orderly existence. His concern is with the *rate* of savings, with the *regularity* of his savings, with the maintenance of his schedule and plan.

Thus, the hoarder watches the balance, while the saver watches the program. The hoarder gloats over the total he has accumulated, while the saver finds pleasure and satisfaction in the weekly or monthly contribution to his savings plan.

With so many institutions available for the purpose of handling the savings of Americans, it is no wonder that there is so much misunderstanding about them.

Generally speaking there are three types of savings banks: mutual savings banks, state-chartered savings banks, and cooperative savings banks (in some states).

These banks perform two basic functions. They take savings deposits and invest them in mortgages, in government bonds, and in selected blue-chip securities. Out of the earnings from investments they pay interest to the depositors.

There are commercial banks of many types. They handle checking accounts, make business loans, personal loans, real-estate loans, and also invest in government bonds and selected securities. They have thrift accounts in which depositors may save their money.

The rate of interest, incidentally, fluctuates from time to time and in different parts of the country.

The Federal Savings and Loan Associations have gained widespread popularity as a refuge for savings during the last fifty years, primarily because they generally pay the highest rates of interest.

Interest rates for the savings banks and commercial banks are regulated by both the Federal Deposit Insurance Corporation and by State Banking Commissions, and they vary from time to time with fluctuations in the economy. When you find it more expensive to borrow money, you will usually find that your savings will command a higher interest rate. Generally speaking, savings banks pay a higher rate of interest on thrift accounts than do commercial banks. However, savings banks offer fewer services. They do not have checking accounts, for instance, nor do they offer a wide variety of personal or commercial loans. Because of a continuing housing boom since World War II, Savings and Loan Associations generally have been able to offer slightly higher interest or dividend payments to their savers than either savings banks or commercial banks.

Most commercial banks do offer you one outstanding advantage. You can arrange for an automatic monthly transfer of a specified sum from your checking account to your savings account. The bank will do it for you. You don't have to worry about it.

The Savings and Loan institutions deal primarily in home mortgages. It is not unusual for them to give higher appraisals, thus to grant higher mortgages on a home than the commercial and savings banks do. They have flourished during a period of tremendous home building in America and, as a result, have offered attractive interest rates to their customers.

In a Savings and Loan plan the saver buys shares which pay the stipulated rate of interest—or, since they're shares, it should be called a dividend, rather than interest. He buys the shares according to a plan, agreeing to a program of regular deposits.

There is no intention, here, to recommend one savings institution more than another. In fact, it makes little difference *where* the money is saved, under this program. It's *how* it's saved. If anyone is foolhardy enough to want to save it under the mattress, that is all right. It seems logical, though, to assume that anyone smart enough to see the value of a good savings program is also smart enough to realize that it's wise to have the saved money in a place where it is insured against loss and where it will earn a little interest.

The main thing is, *Save It!* That's the beginning of independence, of freedom from worry, of security and happiness. Money can't buy everything, but it can make many things more tolerable. Maybe it can't buy happiness, but it can do away with a great deal of unhappiness.

Far too many breadwinners, men and women, go charging

through life, spending their health and sacrificing their home lives on their careers and jobs, just so they can earn more money, without giving much thought to the handling of the money after they've earned it.

For the fact is, very few persons living today can ever earn enough money to gain them independence or retirement. The tax load is too great, the wealth has been too widely distributed to allow for many extra-large salaries.

The person who wants to earn his own independence has but one recourse. He must learn all about the care, cultivation, nurturing, and breeding of money. It's unlikely that he'll ever earn it in large enough amounts—or keep enough of what he earns—to gain his freedom.

So he must learn how to save it. Once he has saved it, he must learn how to invest it.

Unless conditions change greatly, this is the only road for most of us to retirement and security in old age, with worry-free days along the way.

Prudence is a frame of mind that is attained after a decision, the decision to save methodically. It's a decision that's reached in the manner that one decides to stop smoking, for though everyone suspects that smoking is probably detrimental to health, many are unwilling to face up to a decision to stop. That's the way it is with saving. Once the decision is made, once the program is established, it's not difficult to do—and in time it becomes just part of the whole pattern of living.

That's when the saver is started on the road to success and security.

I am certain you know of many fairly well-to-do families that are always in debt, broke, and struggling to make ends meet.

How does it happen?

Take the Smiths and the Joneses, for instance. The Joneses earn $25,000 a year. They live on Maple Street in a home worth $40,000. They have three children. They own a new medium-priced car. Jones never seems to worry about anything. He is relaxed and a good citizen. His bills are up-to-date, he has a savings account, he has a family budget, and he always seems to have cash handy to buy that new camera for himself or an electric train for Junior.

Smith lives across the street from Jones on Maple Street. His basic income is also $25,000. He lives in a $40,000 house, just as Jones does. He has three children, no more and no less expensive than the three Jones children. Smith also owns a new medium-priced car.

Smith is always broke. He is always behind in his bills. He spends most of his spare time doing odd jobs so that he earns, in fact, more than Jones does. Yet there never seems to be anything left over in the Smith household. Smith can't possibly afford the movie camera he has been pricing in the store window. Junior Smith wanted an electric train set like Junior Jones' and Smith had to borrow the money to buy it.

Smith has tried budgeting. He even cut out cigarettes and all the small "drains" on his income. Yet he has never made the grade. The only solution he can think of is to work harder and longer and try to earn more money. But the more he earns, the less he seems to have.

Smith is getting a late start on his problem, but it can be remedied. First, however, he has to find out what's wrong.

It's a safe bet he is having trouble with too much credit—a problem so universal in the United States that it's virtually standardized.

The trouble really started for Smith when he was made assistant sales manager of his company and got his first really important raise—from $15,000 to $18,000. Most people don't regard a $3000 raise as "trouble," but if Smith were truly to analyze his difficulties, he'd agree that his problem dates back to the day his boss so generously recognized his talents and suitably rewarded them.

For that was the night Smith and Mrs. Smith, celebrating, decided they should move into one of those nice new homes on Maple Street, a move which made it necessary for them to buy the new car, not only because of the greater difficulty in commuting but because it became necessary, immediately, to try to keep up with those Joneses across the street.

There's nothing wrong with the American struggle to "keep up with the Joneses." It accounts in significant measure for our national prosperity and full employment. Smith just wasn't ready for for it. He entered a race without preparation. He was a muscular, though untrained, ringside spectator, offering to get into the ring with the skilled champ.

Those $40,000 houses on Maple Street require a $8,000 down payment. Almost any bank in town will take a mortgage for the remainder, ($32,000 or 80%) if you show evidence of stability and seem to have ability to repay.

When Jones bought his house, he had actually saved up nearly $10,000. He had plenty of money for the cash payment, and plenty left over to handle the "closing fees" when the mortgage was drawn and the property deeded over to him, and enough left to handle painlessly the cost of moving.

Smith didn't wait to save any money. He borrowed on his life insurance and on a personal loan to get the $8,000 down payment. So in addition to the mortgage payments, he now pays an additional $250 a month—a full week's pay—on the insurance loan and the personal note.

Naturally he had no money for his new car. He considered himself fortunate that the old car would serve as a down payment, and all he had to do was get a new note with only $110-a-month payments, and he had a new car.

Smith can testify now that this arrangement doesn't work out. He should have waited, as Jones did, until he had accumulated some cash savings. Then he would have been able to handle the new house on Maple Street without so many heartaches.

Now Smith has got to work backward. He must keep his car much longer than his neighbors will probably keep theirs, and he has to live on what will amount to a "starvation budget" for some time, perhaps three years or more, until he gets straightened out.

The trouble with Smith's program at this late date is that all that awaits him at the end of this self-imposed strict regimentation is an ephemeral freedom—freedom from debt—and it will lose most of its allure during Smith's tough struggle. It would have been much better had he imposed the discipline before he moved to Maple Street, for then the goal of the new home, the new neighborhood, would have made it all seem much more worth-while.

The thing to remember—the thing Smith should have remembered—is that living expenses are constant, no matter where you live or how much you earn. These include expenses for shelter, food, utilities, transportation, clothing, medical, dental, recreation, insurance, and various other items.

When you add on to them the payments for several notes and obligations, *plus* the payments on recurring expenses for which you are in arrears, you are in trouble.

A thriving industry has developed in the field of personal finance, where, for a fee, experts take over the job of straightening out people who are in the same mess Smith got into. These outfits exist because the Smiths of the world cannot or will not do the job themselves. It is an amazing commentary on American man to realize that so many topflight businessmen who are noted for their shrewd judgment and sound decisions in the office often leave their personal finances in horrible shape.

To one such firm in New York we brought our typical Mr. Smith. The experts there did not regard Smith as a particular problem or a rarity: he was a typical customer—a debtor, not a breadwinner; a problem, not an individual. Matter of fact, compared to many of the firm's cases, Smith had only an "ordinary" problem.

The experts listed the drains on his income. They found that in addition to living, shelter, utilities, food, transportation, clothing, medical, dental, and recreational expenses, he had eleven separate sets of creditors to whom he was in arrears. These included the auto-finance company, a personal loan from the bank representing the down payment for his home, two more personal loans—one from a small loan company, the other from a credit union (for Junior's electric train)—appliance financing, furniture financing, an FHA Home Improvement Loan, bills for clothing, utilities, medical and dental care, and delinquency payments on his mortgage.

Smith is not untypical.

Chapter 2

Don't Save for a "Rainy Day"

AMERICA'S GREATEST NATURAL RESOURCE IS THE IMPERMANENCE AND instability of her basic economy. It is not, as so many say, the ingenuity and industry of her people. Indeed, Americans *must* be ingenious and industrious and inventive to keep afloat of the great tides of economic change that sweep across the land.

Before the Civil War had ended, the United States was already stepping boldly into an industrial economy. Lee had hardly surrendered when war budgets and emergency finances were forgotten and the people became absorbed with the turbulent eruption of rail and steel empires and the timid beginnings of mass-production techniques which were later refined by Henry Ford.

The Industrial Revolution, economic students called it. And in truth "Revolution" was a mild word. It disrupted the nation's economy to such an extent that whole new concepts had to be formed. Young men left the drudgery of the farm to find more oppressive drudgery in offices and factories.

It was because of the Industrial Revolution that in later years the nation had to set up a system of farm-price supports so that enough people would remain on the farms to supply the industrial areas with food. It was because of the Industrial Revolution that whole new monetary methods were devised—central banking, the Federal Reserve System, a money standard not backed by gold. Social legislation came into being. Securities markets became regulated, as more corporations sought greater amounts of capital through the sale of shares in their businesses.

In the midst of all this, economic students and statisticians, looking calculatingly at the figures recorded by past performances, decided that there was a pattern to prosperity, that there were regular peaks and valleys in their chart lines coming at predictable intervals. Why, they said, it was almost possible to forecast when we'd have prosperity and when we'd have recession.

Thus was born the generation of "cycle worshipers." Everything goes in cycles, they say. Prosperity is a pendulum—push it one way and it must swing back just as far the other way. There have developed refinements and more moderate theories of this basic theme, but it exists, nevertheless, as a common economic belief among a majority of Americans.

It is defeatist thinking, apprehensiveness of the worst kind, for with this brand of "logic" and the dissemination of this type of "knowledge," we have reared a whole nation of cynical pessimists.

I have never been convinced that the theory of cycles is correct. I do not believe in the inevitability of depression. I am willing to be convinced. It is just that I have never seen the theory proved to my satisfaction.

Anyone who believes another depression is inevitable will not be a saver—he'll be a hoarder, and in so being will help to create the very conditions that cause depressions.

He who believes the cycle theory is better off not going into business for himself, for his fears can prevent him from getting the greatest yield in return for the dollars he has invested in his business.

Can we have another depression like the one in the early 30's? Will we return again to the bread lines and soup kitchens, to Okies and CCC camps and 12,800,000 unemployed Americans?

It might not be a bad idea for Americans to take as careful a look at history as the economists have done, to look, for instance, at the history of the utterances of the economists themselves.

Were they right when they said England could not survive off the gold standard? Were they right when they said the first Russian Five Year Plan would fail? Were they right when they said the fluctuation in the stock market in October, 1929, was just a "ripple"? Were they right when they predicted that Hitler could never rearm Germany because there was insufficient gold? Were they right when they said Japan could never afford to wage war because she had insufficient commerce? Were they right when they said that after V-J Day there would be 8,000,000 unemployed Americans?

Because I believe the attitude of the saver is as important as the act of saving, I think it would be wise to re-evaluate some of the deepest beliefs most Americans have about their economy.

Our minds might be less troubled if we took time to appraise the amazing array of safeguards now available to prevent—at least to forestall—any economic catastrophe like the one that followed the 1929 crash.

There are six powerfully effective built-in stabilizers today which were either less effective or not in existence in 1929. These include:

1. The Federal Reserve System, probably the most potent though least understood balance wheel in the economic machine. It can create money, withdraw money from the nation's business lifeline, expand credit or limit it, and it can exert enormous influence on the market for government bonds, those pieces of paper that represent the public indebtedness and public credit of all taxpaying Americans.

2. The Securities and Exchange Commission, which polices

all securities and the stock exchanges, with the result that there are few, if any, worthless stocks offered for sale through the legitimate and established channels such as the New York Stock Exchange or the American Stock Exchange.

3. The Federal Deposit Insurance Corporation, which insures savings and thrift accounts up to $25,000 so that if a bank should fail—and what an unusual event these days—the depositors will get their money intact.

4. The Council of Economic Advisers established by the Full Employment Act of 1946. It is the duty of the Council to detect the threat of recession or indications of inflation and to recommend to the President counteractive measures.

5. Unemployment Compensation, the state-controlled setup for supplying income to those who have been laid off.

6. The Social Security Administration, which aids an increasing number of Americans who have reached retirement age or are incapable of earning their own living.

One by one, step by step, these devices have been built into the national structure. Each one functions. Each has been put to the test. Each is hair-triggered to go into action when needed.

The Federal Reserve Board, for instance, is as vigilant as a fo'cas'le lookout at midnight. Its activities seldom rate the front pages, yet it provides fully as much "protection" as the police departments or the FBI. The Fed's functions are almost exclusively aimed at protecting the dollars of all Americans, no matter what their income, station, or calling.

The Fed stands alert, sampling the economic weather, an eye always on its barometric statistics. When it spots a recession brewing, it can pump money into the economy as ballast against the storm. When the skies get too fair, the seas too calm, and the winds fall off, the weather-watching Fed determines if we're heading into a period of inflation and, if so, pumps money out of the economy to lighten the load.

The pump is geared into the Fed's required reserve fund. By raising or lowering the reserve required of its 7000 member banks, it can create money which will be circulated among the people, stimulating prosperity, or it can freeze the money in cold storage, neutralizing the effect of inflation.

Unless you follow the financial pages of your newspaper you may not recall that in 1948, when inflation appeared to get out of hand, the Fed removed $3,000,000,000 from circulation merely by issuing three separate reserve-raising orders to its member banks. The banks had to keep that much more money in their reserve accounts. There was that much *less* money to be loaned.

Actually the effect was far greater than the $3,000,000,000 frozen in the reserve funds.

If the same orders were issued today, Fed officials figure that every $1000 in the reserve account represents $5000 in bank loans. For every dollar a bank has in reserve, it can lend about $5.00. Thus, the $3,000,000,000 added to reserves actually removed about $15,000,000,000 from the economy, which would have taken the form of loans to businesses, farmers, and others.

It's certainly an easy and effective way to control inflation.

The principle works just as well and just as effectively in reverse. When the Fed detects a sloughing-off in the economy, it "frees" some of its reserve money and the same ratio obtains.

Early in 1954, when things looked gloomy to the Fed's statisticians, an order was issued lowering reserve requirements. It had the effect of slowing the business decline.

Another move in the spring of 1954 was the lowering of the "discount rate" by the Federal Reserve. That meant that member banks could borrow from the Fed at a lower cost, hence were encouraged to make more loans. The Fed, in effect, "sells" money to its member banks. When it lowers the discount rate, it means that it is taking a smaller profit margin, and when the member banks pay off the bill, at some future date, they have had the benefit of a bargain.

The Fed's way of "buying the money back," figuratively, is to raise reserve requirements. In the inflationary period of 1969–1972 the Fed raised both the reserve requirements and the discount rate several times. As a result you read that banks were raising their "prime rate," which is the interest charged to their most creditworthy customers, such as blue chip corporations. Following right along behind this boost in the prime rate was an increase in interest rates charged to less creditworthy customers, such as individuals who wanted to take out loans to buy cars, improve their homes or consolidate their bills.

In its simplest form, the bank structure is like any other industry. The Federal Reserve "manufactures" the money and sells it at a specified markup (on time payments, of course) to member banks. The banks, like retailers or middle men, then sell the money to borrowers at an added markup.

But since money is the root of all commerce, the Fed is in a position to stimulate or impose a drag on the economy, whichever may be needed to maintain relatively smooth sailing.

If the Federal Reserve may be regarded as the fo'cas'le watch, then the guard on the flying bridge, scanning the entire horizon, is the staff of the President's Economic Adviser. It's a guard armed with thick-lensed powerful binoculars and hypersensitive radarlike devices for detecting that which is not yet visible.

There are over 800 various statistical measures such as steel production, kilowatt-hour production, car-loadings, stock averages, imports, cotton spindles in place, wheatcrop yield, and the like. The staff of the Economic Adviser watches them all. Like the Fed, it has developed certain ones which it regards as more sensitive, more barometrical. Its job is to detect the presence of recession or inflation and to work up stand-by plans which can be invoked at a certain point.

The existing stand-by plan for recession is no different from the one employed by President Roosevelt in the mid-30's after it was developed by England's "pump-priming" economist, Lord Keynes. It's simply the commencement of a huge government-spending program to pump money into the economy.

The Adviser's main job is to see that there is a high level of employment. Even through the several periods of prosperity in the last two decades, the Adviser found it necessary to advise that certain government contracts be channeled to particular areas where some cities were put on the "critical list" because of unemployment.

These are man-made stabilizers, built into our government to help us avoid another '29 crash.

There is natural strength, however, which is perhaps even more important to our future economic health. For America's economy is like a tree. In the years since '29 it has grown stronger, sturdier, more impervious to damage.

This is why it's good to look at history in clear perspective. In it, the troubled mind can find solace.

Regard these historical facts:

National income is estimated at more than 900% higher than it was in 1929, $795,887,000,000 as opposed to $87,400,000,000.

Is this just "inflation," as the pessimists say?

Hardly, for the Gross National Product, the total output of goods and services, is up by more than 900% also ($975,000,-000,000 as opposed to $103,800,000,000).

The disposable income of Americans before taxes is up 1000%. Earnings of all types is up between 800% and 900%.

Yet it costs only about 85% more to live than it did in 1929.

Consumer wealth is estimated in the United States as more than a *trillion* dollars.

This compares with offsetting debts in the neighborhood of $300,000,000,000.

Half the families in America have net worth of $10,000 or more.

Nearly a fourth of all families own more than $30,000 in net assets.

Four fifths of those who earn under $7,000 a year own nearly half the nation's wealth (see the pyramid drawings on page 25).

And we're growing fast.

From about 1948 until 1972 the economists and statisticians watched the zooming birth rate, some with satisfaction, some with apprehension. They figured correctly that by the year 1970 we would have a consuming population of 200,000,000 in America. In 1972, perhaps because of the pill and liberalized abortions, the birth rate dropped until it reached zero-growth—no more babies were being born than there were adults dying off.

Was it all as terrible and frightening as some statisticians had led you to believe?

These new little Americans are consumers all. They'll need food, clothing, shelter, and gadgets, and will, by their very existence, cause employment and production.

In some countries they'd pose a problem. But not in the United States, for within the framework of the free-enterprise system America has built up a unique version of capitalism—a system with the built-in components of success. Ours is not a system of conservation, nor merely a system of production. Ours is a nation of buyers and suppliers. The more we buy the more we have to supply. Thus is created more employment which leads to more buying, and so on.

I saw a 1955 report by a United Nations committee which said that the world birth rate was so rapid that by the year 2000 or so we would have difficulty feeding all the mouths.

Of course we would, if our crop yields remained the same as they are today, if farming and agriculture and animal husbandry didn't advance a whit between 1955 and the year 2000. But who, looking at the progress of man in the fields of science in the past three decades, can *believe* that we're going to be stagnant, just breeders of children, during that forty-five year-period?

It's a good bet that the fathers of these UN purveyors warned Henry Ford not to build so many cars because there weren't enough roads to hold them all.

Some of us, as savers, worry about inflation and the seemingly constant erosion of the value of our saved dollars. We are prone to say it's silly to save a dollar worth 49 cents on a 1929 basis, and then take it out and use it fifteen years later when it's worth, perhaps, only 35 cents.

Don't let the statistics fool you.

In the first place, this is nothing new. All monetary values have been decreasing since time began. It is inevitable, except for brief periods.

When there's a depression, money buys more. But when the depression ends, it resumes its steady devaluation.

There's no such thing as a "normal" economy; it never stands still long enough to establish a norm. It's silly for economic students to wish for "things to return to normal." There's no such condition.

But for the sake of comparison, the statisticians compute the average purchasing power of a dollar for the years 1935–39 as being equal to 100 cents. In other words—just for the establishment of a basis—a 1935–39 average dollar was worth a dollar.

So let's look again at the history books for more solace.

Back in 1929—that boom year, remember—average hourly earnings were 56 cents. Based on that average dollar of 1935–39, the real hourly earnings were 77 cents. In other words, 56 cents' worth of pay bought 77 cents' worth of goods and services.

In 1953 the average hourly earnings were $1.76. Based on that same average 1935–39 dollar, the real hourly earnings were $1.56. Or, $1.76 worth of pay bought $1.56 worth of goods and services.

After *deducting* the inflation, after figuring for the loss in purchasing power of the dollar, there has still been a 126 per cent increase in average hourly earnings of American industrial workers since 1929. A *real* increase.

Inflation hasn't been able to keep up with the economic growth. So what is normal? I submit that it's better to receive $1.76 that is really worth only $1.56 than it is to receive 56 cents that's worth 77 cents. Even though today you receive in *real* money *less* than you actually earn, whereas in earlier days you received in *real* money *more* than you actually earned, you're better off with today's earnings.

Again, in 1967, for the fourth time since the Market Crash of 1929* the Bureau of Labor Statistics of the Department of Labor

*See *The Day The Market Crashed,* by Donald I. Rogers, Arlington House, 1971.

revised the index base for calculating purchasing power of the dollar. This time the dollar of 1967 equals $1.00. Thus, the value of dollars dating from 1940 through 1970 (to June 30, 1971) are evaluated as follows (fractions of cents omitted):

1940	$2.38	1960	$1.13
1950	1.39	1961	1.12
1951	1.29	1962	1.10
1952	1.26	1963	1.09
1953	1.25	1964	1.08
1954	1.24	1965	1.06
1955	1.25	1966	1.03
1956	1.23	1967	1.00
1957	1.19	1968	0.96
1958	1.16	1969	0.91
1959	1.15	1970	0.86

All statistics are drab and make dull reading. But I believe that those figures set forth in the preceding paragraphs of this chapter are about as exciting as any that can be compiled.

Their purpose is to persuade the timid that a savings program is wise, that "economic factors" will not prevail to spoil all plans. I seek only to show that: *1.* It is unlikely that we will have another depression; and *2.* Dollars that are saved will not be drastically diluted by inflation.

At this point we are discussing only the need for saving regularly. In later chapters we will consider what to do with some portions of the savings—how to hedge against inflation or recession; how to invest so your purchasing power will remain relatively stable and constant. For there is no denying that inflation—that devaluation of the dollar—will continue.

But most of us are too apprehensive about another depression. We have been too ready to subscribe to the theory of the cycles, to the belief that the pendulum always swings back.

It is well not to forget that principal feature of our economy, the fact that we are suppliers and buyers, that spending is what makes our economy function, what makes us prosperous.

This prosperity doesn't depend on Uncle Sam's largess, either, for no matter how much the government spends, the consumers manage to dwarf the effort. Consumers spend much more than business and government combined—nearly three quarters of the total national spending.

As long as this keeps up, as long as Americans want new cars, homes, appliances, clothes, and "things," our prosperity will continue.

Back in 1945 we entered the Atomic Age. But we have barely explored the potentials of the Chemical Age or the Electronic Age, both of which antedate atomic energy.

Ahead of us? Economically speaking there can be nothing but tremendous achievements in glamorous new fields, unless humanity finds it cannot exist without war. A depression's the last thing to fear.

Chapter 3

Savings in Real Estate

PROBABLY NO ONE HAS EVER BOUGHT A HOUSE WITHOUT BELIEVING HE was making an "investment," as well as buying the structure of a home.

Throughout the years a majority of these "investors" were wrong. They had made unprofitable investments or profitless ones in which they broke even.

On the other hand I know of a man who sold his house and moved seven times in eight years, each time at a delightful profit, and at the time of this writing resides in a house that is much desired by prospective buyers. After all his profitable moves he has nearly 100 per cent equity in it. There's but a small mortgage.

Buying a house appeals to the logic. It usually seems like a guaranteed good investment. The reasoning generally runs something like this: We have to pay rent anyway. Might as well pay off on a mortgage. Then, instead of giving our money to a landlord, we're in reality paying it to ourselves. Can't go far wrong; after all, the bank will be putting up anywhere from 60 to 80 per cent of the money. And if the bank approves the mortgage, it means the bank's appraisers have found it to be a "good" house, worthy of investment . . .

What may be a good investment for a bank may not always be a good investment for an individual. It depends whether you're lending the money with the expectation of being paid back, with interest, at regular intervals, or whether you're borrowing the money and, by paying it back, buying a larger and larger equity in the house. It should be remembered that with each payment the borrower makes on his mortgage, the bank owns a smaller equity in the house.

The bank doesn't have to care whether a $20,000 house will be worth $20,000 in twenty years when the mortgage is paid in full. That's the worry of the buyer.

In fact, assuming that the borrower has asked for a $20,000 mortgage on a house worth $30,000 to be paid off in monthly amortization payments over a twenty-year period, the bank, acting in the interests of its own business and in behalf of its own stockholders, thinks *just the opposite* of the "investor" who is borrowing the money.

The bank asks itself: Will this house be worth $15,000 in five years? For in five years a quarter of the mortgage will have been paid back, and the bank's concern is only whether it would have trouble getting $15,000 for the place in five years. Or $10,000 in ten years; or $5,000 in fifteen years.

In a great many of the postwar (post-World War II, that is) houses, where the banks granted mortgages for 60 to 65 percent of the appraised value of the house with twenty-year terms, the banks figured on breaking even considerably before half the time has elapsed. Counting interest paid on the loan the resale value of the house, the banks recovered their loan and safely secured the balance long before the first ten years of the mortgage's life. The same principle obtains today.

Banks have not always acted wisely in this respect, and this may be why some of them are hypercautious. During the recession of late 1953 and early 1954 a great many bankers decided to become cautious about granting mortgages—"selective," they call it, an exceptionally graphic term for the banking vocabulary.

Houses which in 1950 had been worth $15,000, and on which banks had made loans of $11,500, were resold in that recessed 1953–54 period without much help from the banks. In the three years since 1950 the mortgages had been paid off to about $9800 —and that's *all* the banks would lend on new mortgages when the houses were resold.

Again in the "tight money" periods of 1966–67 and 1969–70, the banks over-reacted to the mortgage market and added gloom to a slump by drying up the home building industry, simply by holding back on mortgage money. It must be remembered that, in banking, mortgages are not considered the best investments, because defaulted mortgages push banks into the real estate business, where they are unaccustomed to operating and ill-equipped to function. This is why savings banks and savings and loan associations dominate the mortgage market.

Caution? Perhaps, but one might wonder at the wisdom of deliberately depressing the value of houses in whole areas, when the *banks themselves* owned millions of dollars of equity —unpaid balances in existing mortgages—in those homes.

The advent of the monthly amortization plan, a relatively recent development, has made it possible for almost everyone to save through real estate.

Until about 25 years ago mortgages were granted for small percentages of total appraised value. A borrower was lucky, indeed, if he could get a mortgage for 40 per cent of the total value of his home. But he was not required to pay off the mortgage. He got the money and agreed only to pay the interest on it, usually annually. True, it was a callable note, but banks rarely called them.

It was the Savings and Loan Associations, working out a system of painless home-ownership for their members, that developed the monthly amortization mortgage. It has, today, become the standard mortgage.

Because of it more Americans than ever are buying their own homes. In 1951, for the first time since the Industrial Revolution following the Civil War, more than half the families of America lived in their own homes. A good deal of the credit for this can go to the Savings and Loan Associations for perfection of the "easy payment" mortgages. The ratio of home ownership still exists.

It can be assumed with relative confidence that most of these homes are good properties to own—as homes. It is too bad that there are not figures to show how many of them are good investments, how many of them, in the long haul, will increase in value rather than devaluate with the general depreciation of aging structures.

It would be handy for potential home buyers to know just what it was that made the difference between buying a house for a home and buying a house for investment.

This should not imply that houses bought for investment are not necessarily houses that make good homes. The two features are cordially compatible. There are many grand homes that are also good investments—splendid abodes for the hard-won savings of thoughtful couples.

There *is* logic in buying a house as a means of "forced" savings. It *does* provide a repository for a certain "saved" amount of monthly "rent." A home owner is, indeed, paying his money to himself rather than to a landlord—*plus* interest to a bank, *plus* taxes, *plus* insurance, *plus* upkeep, *plus* improvement.

It's these *plus* factors that are sometimes overlooked and frequently upset family savings plans. A great many of them have not had sufficient upkeep.

The bank lending the money on the mortgage insists that there be fire insurance and liability insurance sufficient to cover the *unpaid* balance of the mortgage, a balance which is reduced usually on monthly terms. Many ex-GIs have not taken into account the fact that the insurance carried on their homes today is much less than the insurance they carried five, eight, or ten years ago when the house was purchased. Many, too, fail to realize that in the event of fire, it may be only the bank that is protected.

Even those who have given consideration to this feature and have added to their own fire insurance coverage, over and above the amount of the unpaid mortgage balance, have, frequently, failed to take into consideration the two most important "investment" factors of their property: 1. The increased resale value of the home, or appreciation; and 2. The improvements they have made during the years.

Yet, despite the rather wide-scale negligence and irresponsibility among home owners, it is my belief that the only sensible way to conduct a complete and rewarding savings program is through home-ownership and/or some kind of investment in real estate.

It is a certainty that in the years ahead millions of American families will move into their own homes for the first time and that additional millions of families will sell the homes they are occupying and buy new ones as their families grow or their financial capacities change.

What should a buyer look for in selecting a home that will also be a good investment?

First, and quite naturally, price.

There has grown in America a mighty force of snobbishness around the real estate market. It is almost essential to personal success or business success to have a good, an acceptable, address. This is not evil; it was inevitable. As our metropolitan centers grow more crowded and as our suburban areas become more urban, the development of neighborhoods and communities around home values and income levels is natural.

This is a wholesome situation. No one wants a $50,000 home beside a $15,000 bungalow. The occupants of the bungalow would feel uneasy and the owner of the $50,000 home would worry about the depreciation of his property values because of the manner of maintenance or lack of maintenance of the abutting properties.

It is not un-American to think along these lines. The generations born since the New Deal have heard a great deal about the evils of concentrated wealth, the sins of the rich, and the nobility of the poor. The long, wretched depression years fertilized the seedlings of this generalized philosophy and they grew and flourished. Certainly the possession of money shouldn't make a person more acceptable, nor does it indicate, in itself, that he is a superior person. However, in *most* cases, the presence of a high income indicates that its owner has equipped himself better and worked harder than many of those with less income. This is true, so let's face it. It's extremely difficult today, because of taxes, to inherit much money, so that most high incomes are *earned* incomes, and the earner is entitled to the benefits of his labor.

There are notable exceptions, of course. Such measures cannot be made against many persons, including clergymen or teachers or even newspapermen, most of whom are dedicated souls, held, by their dedication, aloof from material rewards.

But when it comes to buying real estate, it pays to be practical and to forget old resentments and worn theories about the end results of the capitalistic system.

My advice is to buy as much as you can possibly afford. Never less.

Never buy a house because the required down payment happens to coincide with how much you have saved and are prepared to give as a down payment. Forget the down payment and think only of the monthly carrying charge—or amortization charge.

Re-evaluate the family budget. Find out the *maximum* you could pay each month for rent. If it's $300, deduct 15 per cent for the amount you should set aside to maintain the home, and the balance—$255—is the amount you can afford for monthly mortgage amortization payments.

If your budget would stand a monthly rent of $500, you figure it the same, except you deduct only 10 per cent. In other words, you can afford to pay $450 monthly to the bank and will save $50 monthly for upkeep of the house.

Naturally these are rule-of-thumb calculations and cannot apply wholesale. They'll come out remarkable close in most situations, however. They're based on the conventional mortgage in use today where the bank requires a monthly payment which is split to cover: one twelfth the annual payment on principal; one twelfth the annual interest charge; one twelfth of the annual estimated tax bill; one twelfth of the annual insurance bill; one twelfth of the annual water bill; one twelfth of an annual escrow account, a reserve for contingencies in case the taxes are higher than expected.

Naturally, if the bank does not deal in this type of mortgage, if, for instance, it does not make provisions for taxes and water levies; you will have to reckon them into your own plans.

If such a mortgage is obtainable, and it should be, figure it roughly this way:

What you can afford for monthly "rent". $300.00
Less 15 per cent.. 45.00

    Balance $255.00
Thus:
Amount you can afford to pay for monthly
    amortization charges $255.00
Amount you should save monthly for up-
    keep 45.00
Or annually
      Total to bank $3060.00
      Total for upkeep 540.00

      Total cost to you $3600.00

So, first it is determined how much you can afford—the *maximum* you can afford—in monthly amortization payments.

The next step is to go to a bank and get a mortgage "schedule." Find out how they compute their monthly amortization charges. Find out how much interest they charge. Find out whether they grant fifteen-year, twenty-year, or twenty-five-year mortgages.

The bank can give you a pretty good idea of the system used by it so that you can figure out for yourself how big your mortgage should be. For instance, should it be a $12,000 mortgage? Or $15,000, or what?

Or, you can go to a bank and "lay it on the line." Tell the man in the mortgage department that you've figured it out, you can afford $255.00 per month for mortgage payments, and you want to know how much of a mortgage that will buy you.

Only until you're armed with this information should you house hunt.

Otherwise, you won't get the best deal. You'll buy less than you can afford, or more than you can afford. Such an important step shouldn't be left to luck.

It is the practice for commercial banks, savings banks, and mortgage companies to lend a maximum of 60 per cent to 70 per cent of the appraised value of a house—*their* appraisal, that is. The Federal Savings and Loan Associations, because they are primarily in the real estate financing business, frequently lend up to 80 per cent.

This doesn't mean that if a commerical bank is willing to lend an acceptable applicant $6000 on a house appraised at $10,000, it would lend $6000 on the house next to it which is appraised at $8000. The procedure for lending money on mortgages is much different from the procedure for making personal loans. The borrower doesn't establish a so-called "line of credit" or credit rating. It's the value of the house *plus* the ability of the borrower to repay that determines the willingness of the bank to issue a mortgage, and the leading role in the decision is played by the appraiser's report of the house.

Bear this in mind as you shop for a home: The bank's appraiser is the fellow who will have the most to say about whether you get your mortgage. He's really your friend, if he's a professional man who knows his business—and most are;

though I'll admit that I've seen some mighty fuzzy amateurs in the smaller banks. The professional appraiser will look for all the flaws in the house, the location, the title, and will give a professional opinion as to whether the buyer is making a wise purchase.

An ethical real estate agency can also be of help. The agents do not charge a fee of the buyers. They get a percentage of the selling price from the seller. A community or neighborhood agent can let you know about trends in certain localities, whether cheap or shabby construction is likely to develop in the area, whether undesirable elements of the population are moving nearby. He can tell you about schools, churches, transportation, availability of shopping facilities. These are elemental things. Most of all, he can tell you about the investment potential of the home you hope to buy—whether the population trend is in that direction, whether property values in that area have been in the ascendency, if the style, the construction of the house is the kind that will be in demand in that area in the years to come.

All these factors should be weighed in a decision to buy a home:

Fundamentally, is it the very best home you can afford to buy? Is it the very best location available? Is it the best community in your price range?

In searching for the "best" it's easy to get gouged by sharp dealers. Because of location some homes are sold with outrageous price tags on them. I have seen one house, built from a standard architectural plan available through the Federal Housing Administration, have three widely varying prices in three separate suburbs of New York City. A six-room, one and one-half bath, Dutch Colonial-type house, almost identical in each instance, sold for $20,000 on Long Island's South Shore, $30,000 on Long Island's North Shore, and $43,500 in Westchester County. The difference in plots on which the houses were built hardly justified the difference in price. At most the value for the land couldn't have ranged more than $3500 to $4000.

So "neighborhood" is worth something to the investor. Is the

Westchester neighborhood worth $23,500 more than the South Shore neighborhood?

It's highly doubtful. Someplace in between $20,000 and $43,-500 there's a sensible, efficient, practical price.

Arty discussions of architecture are impractical and consideration of artistic architecture is expensive. Purchase of a home with unique or unusual or ultra-modernistic architectural features should not be considered an investment—it's speculation. The place may be worth more in years to come, but it probably won't.

Americans have a fetish for "trade-ins" and generally feel uncomfortable in a car more than three years old. They have even allowed this national characteristic to invade the home so that bathroom fixtures have to be of recent vintage, else the hostess is apologetic when guests use the plumbing. It's sensible to spend money on genuine improvements; not so sensible to spend it solely for styling. This holds true with kitchen appliances as well.

It is easy to allow the desire for style and modishness to influence the selection of a home. Common sense will dictate where useful improvement in architectural design leaves off and where mere stylishness begins. The ranch-type home is sensible if it isn't sprawled over too wide an area, for it eliminates stair-climbing. But in some areas of the North, the owner of a ranch-type home may awaken one spring or fall morning to find nearly a quarter-inch of moisture covering the floor that has no cellar under it. There's heavy condensation when the days are hot and the nights are much cooler.

Nor is it wise to let a current "trend" dictate choice of a home. A few years ago large houses were white elephants. Today they're in brisk demand. A few years ago people were looking for extreme snugness in homes—the tinier the kitchen, the more compact storage space. Today they're looking for more room to move around in. The advent of television turned homes into living quarters rather than mere sleeping-and-eating places.

Another thing we Americans are prone to do is to regard as

normal and standard those things which are acceptable or pleasing or necessary to us as individuals. Not a bad trait, really, but it's one to eschew when buying real estate. The fact that your income improves, allowing you to move from an inexpensive home into a more palatial one, doesn't mean that the market in inexpensive homes is ended. Or if an increase in the size of family makes it advisable to move from a small home into a larger one, it doesn't mean that there will not be a continuing market for smaller homes.

Trends, as such, are not too important in home investment; that is, trends to size or style or layout. A home finished with stucco isn't necessarily a dated home and perforce less desirable in the resale market, just because stucco is no longer so widely used.

Some of the foregoing admonitions may sound unimportant. But they are common characteristcs or attitudes that are responsible in many instances for limiting the investment potential of home purchases.

The well-managed family will accomplish three things when it buys and moves into a house: it will get a home; it will inaugurate a system of forced savings; and it will create a good investment. A wisely selected house will offer these three things.

What, then, are the ground rules, the safety rules, for buying a home that is also an investment?

Find out how much you can spend each month on amortization charges.

Conduct your search among houses and in neighborhoods that are the best you can afford. Even "reach" a little, if you have to.

Check the zoning laws. Make sure commercial or industrial enterprises won't spoil the neighborhood.

Check the community's Master Plan so you'll be sure there isn't a program to build a super-highway through your living room in ten years' time.

Check the transportation, schools, churches, shopping facilities.

Check the sewage system. Is there a city sewer? Or cesspools?

Find out about the source of water and its cost.

Ask yourself: Is this a stabilized, established area that will improve, will be a better place to live as time goes on?

Check, if you can, the general income levels of the families in the neighborhood, their cultural and educational levels, too.

Is the police protection adequate? What does the insurance company feel about the fire protection?

Look beyond your neighborhood at the entire community. Is it a good community, of good reputation? Make sure you're not moving into an oasis in a veritable desert. A bad town can pull down your values despite all the efforts of the folks in your immediate neighborhood.

Ask the bank's appraiser to give you specifics on the condition of the chimneys, the foundation, the plumbing and heating, the wiring, the roof. For instance, condition of the water may determine whether copper tubing is preferable to brass piping. The appraiser will know about this. You can check some things for yourself. The joists—beams—in the basement's ceiling should not be less than 8-x-2's spaced so that it measures no more than fifteen inches from the center of one joist to the center of another. If there is a variance, find out why.

Common sense tells you that plaster walls and ceilings are more valuable than those made of plasterboard or other prefabricated materials. You can see for yourself whether the place needs paint. With a pocketknife you can check the condition of the wood at danger spots like window sills and doorsills.

Above all, don't stand on ceremony or be overly polite when inspecting a house. Remember: it's going to be *your* money that buys it, and no matter what the asking price may be—it's a *lot* of money, to anybody.

Once the house has been selected and the mortgage approved, there are two important and absolutely necessary steps: 1. Retain a competent, experienced lawyer, one who has had experience with real estate transactions. 2. Either retain a title guarantee company or *insist* that the seller furnish you with a guaranteed title.

A buyer is reckless and foolhardy who does not do both of these things.

A mortgage closing is a weird ceremony to those who have never witnessed it; and the uninitiate attending without legal counsel will find himself listening to gibberish in a foreign language which, even with explanation, can mean little to him. He will be asked to sign agreements and documents that he does not fully understand. Among other things, there will be prorated settlements on such things as water bills, taxes, the amount of fuel oil remaining in the tank, the unused portion of the insurance policies. Only a lawyer can represent a buyer efficiently at a time like this.

If the bank operates efficiently it will insist on a guaranteed title. It is advisable to check this first. But if it does not so insist, then the buyer should arrange to have one.

A title guarantee company will survey the property, definitely establish the lines, and then search the deeds and records, check the plot maps, and make sure that the seller *has the right* to convey title to you. Once the title is cleared, the company *guarantees* to you that it is all right to buy it—and, to protect you, the company *insures* the title. In other words, once the company guarantees the title, your investment is safe, for if for any reason the title is questioned and found to be unsalable, you'll get your money back from the title guarantee company.

Remember, a seller is not required to give proof of ownership. That's the buyer's worry. The ancient precept, *"Caveat Emptor"*—let the buyer beware!—still exists in law.

Another thing to remember is that these closing fees, charges for the lawer, the title guarantee company, the unused fuel, the unused portion of insurance policies, and the unexpended portion of prepaid taxes and water bills will have to be settled at the time of closing the mortgage. Under the convential FHA-guaranteed mortgage, you will also be required to set up some sort of "escrow account" with the bank. It's not safe to go to a mortgage closing with less than $500 to $1,000 available for paying bills and setting up the escrow. Your lawyer should advise you, in advance, just how much this will be.

Anyone who has studied real estate procedures may realize that I have ignored the basic rules of the Federal Housing Administration in suggesting how much can be spent on monthly amortization charges. This is because I believe the FHA has been unrealistic about it, a belief that is shared by a growing number of bankers.

Many may recall the old traditional yardstick—carrying costs on a home should not exceed one quarter of a breadwinner's annual income. Included in carrying costs were practically everything: rent (or mortgage), taxes, water, light, phone, insurance, fuel, repairs, household help, laundry, interest.

It just doesn't work, particularly for the lower-income families. Their payments for these services are naturally a much higher percentage of their annual income than the payments of the more fortunate. Adherence to this rule would condemn many families to living in hovels.

I believe that hard-and-fast rules are unwise. Furthermore, I have always resented having a bank tell me how much I can afford to spend for a mortgage or for anything else. I believe that's a matter for personal decision. Some people may prefer a cheap house, but an expensive car, ambitious insurance program, and extraordinary educations for their children. Others may want a luxury home at the pain of driving an old car and skimping on swank clothes.

It seems to me that a person of normal intelligence can work out his own budget and determine just how much he can afford to spend for shelter. Furthermore, I believe that he should spend the maximum, not the minimum, for that is part of the savings and investment program I intend to unfold. Creation of a family budget is not hard. Numerous books have been written about it to give easily understood guides. A particularly good one, in my opinion, is *Managing Your Money,* by the late tax expert J. K. Lasser and the financial expert Sylvia F. Porter.*

If a borrower prepares himself before he goes to the bank, he

*Published by Henry Holt and Company, New York, 1953.

can usually get a reasonable audience with the mortgage officer. If he is unprepared, the banker will be forced to protect his bank and its stockholders by sticking to the old rules and telling the borrower just how much he can afford.

The most useful documents a borrower can bring with him are: *1.* A history of employment and history of income, along with an appraisal of future income; and *2.* A statement of net worth.

To work out such a statement is not difficult.

List all your assets: the market value of your car; the market value of any property or possessions you own; the total of your savings; the market value of your securities; the cash-surrender value of your insurance; the resale value of your furniture, appliances, and tools—and *list* them.

Against these, list your liabilities: any unpaid balances on notes to banks or other lenders, plus all other encumbrances.

Subtract the total liabilities from the total assets. That's your net worth, or at least it's a workable "net worth" adequate for your purpose.

Up to this point we have been discussing the purchase of homes in established neighborhoods. All over the nation, however, on the outskirts of metropolitan centers there have sprung up tremendous areas of new homes; development communities, bedroom towns for commuters.

There is no reason why the same rules stated in the foregoing cannot apply to the purchase of one of these homes. There are added precautions that must be taken, however.

Many of these "developments" are in unincorporated areas or in districts that have not been accepted officially by the city or township in which they're located. It is necessary to check on such things as sewage facilities, street lights, sidewalks, garbage collection, grading and surfacing of the streets, street-drainage catch basins, and the like.

There may be added special assessments for these facilities and services. The fact that there's a nicely paved and surfaced street going past the house doesn't mean, necessarily, that the street has been accepted by the town or city; and the owner of the house may find, someday, that he has to chip in with his neighbors to get the snow plowed off and the tar put back on. Or he may find that once the street is accepted, he's required to pay a special assessment for curbing or catch-basin drains.

A major point to bear in mind is this: Most of these development homes are built from the same general floor plan and sell in the same general price range. No matter how much one property owner may spend to improve and beautify his home, its resale value will be not much more than the general resale value of all the rest of the homes in the development.

The addition of a $5000 swimming pool will not boost the resale price of a development home by $5000. Bank appraisals are set for the whole district, and the prospective buyer wouldn't be able to borrow $5000 more to take into account the swimming pool, which would mean he'd have to have $5000 cash *in addition to* the required down payment. A person with that kind of money for a down payment would probably rather spend it on a home that wasn't so rigidly classified as to price level.

The *real* investor in a home may want to build his own.

This is a long-range project, one calling for wise and expert counsel and assistance. There are the selection of a plot, the careful consultation of the zoning laws, the knotty and complicated conferences with architects and contractors to consider.

Most important is the fact that it's unprofitable to build a cheap or inexpensive home. Surveys show that unless a person can afford a rather expensive structure, he's better off and will get more value for his money if he buys a home that's already built. If it's a new home, it was probably built with mass-production techniques and its hardware and fixtures were bought in wholesale lots so that the saving might be passed along to the buyer. It's certainly not as good as a home built to individual specifications. But in the low and medium price range, it's a wiser dollar-for-dollar investment.

Another point to bear in mind is that a much larger amount of cash is needed to build your own home. There are many more "extra" charges in creating a new house, charges which have been paid and discounted in an existing house. Also, banks are more cautious about lending money on new homes; the place can't be appraised, unforeseen events might pop up —in effect, the bank is being asked to finance a pig in a poke.

Unless a person knows a good deal about contracts and construction, he should not attempt to deal directly with the contractors.

There are many highly ethical and trustworthy contractors, of course. But there are many who are not. Unless there can be *complete* trust and confidence in a contractor, the buyer should see that there is constant supervision of the construction and someone to check on strict adherence to the specifications of the contract.

It's easy, these days, to buy for a dollar or two, the complete plans for a home. Since it has to be an accepted fact that the builder of a new home is going to pay considerably more than he would otherwise, it seems to me more practical to have the plans drawn to meet individual requirements and preferences.

A reliable and ethical architectural firm will draw the plans —and redraw them, if necessary—to meet the desires of the prospective builder and his family, then will draw up specifications for the contractor such as the degree of grade on the lawn, the sand-cement-gravel mixture in the concrete, the type of plumbing, the type of nails, the type of gutters at the eaves, the kind of wiring, etc. After that the architect will *supervise* the construction and see to it that the terms of the contract and the specifications are being observed.

For this service, architects charge from 3 per cent to 10 per cent or more of the total cost.

But before an architect is consulted, a lawyer has to be given the assignment of making it all legal. He has to check the zoning laws, check the easements (or restrictions) of the area, see to the surveying and establishment of boundary lines to avoid encroachment, get a clear and guaranteed title, help set up the financing with the bank or lender, and assist in the preparation of the construction contract.

One thing to count on: building a new home will cost more than you expected it would, unless you're exceptionally liberal in making allowances in your plans.

There is one other type of home that must be considered in a study of this kind, the cooperative apartment. It may be absolutely essential that a person live in the heart of the city. Perhaps his work or other considerations prohibit the life of a commuter. He has no choice but to live in an apartment, one which he rents or one which he owns on a cooperative basis.

Buying a cooperative is risky. It calls for careful preliminary investigation. The rules, the precautions necessary in buying a private dwelling, are perhaps more essential in the purchase of a cooperative apartment. Beyond doubt the buyer is venturing into the field of real estate speculation.

If all of the other apartments in the building have not been sold to financially responsible persons, you may get stuck with some unexpected charges which will be mandatory upon you if only to protect your own investment.

The only advice that can be given to the prospective buyer of an apartment in a cooperative apartment house is, *investigate thoroughly*. Find out the extent of your responsibility in every contingency.

Some cooperatives have high mortgages, requiring but small down payment from the buyers. Others do not have such high mortgages and a comparatively high down payment is necessary.

If I were to buy in a cooperative, I'd look for the ones with low mortgages, the ones which demand a substantial down payment from the occupants. This would indicate, to some extent, at least, the ability of your business partners (for that's what the other occupants are) to assume financial responsibility. Then I'd have an expert appraiser go over the property to make sure that the low mortgage didn't indicate a bank's unwillingness to lend money on the place because of inferior construction or some other problem.

In New York City, Chicago, Philadelphia, and other large cities there are also attached homes in the "brownstone" tradition. These, too, are to be considered for home investment. But the precautionary rules should apply rigidly. There should be a comprehensive report on the neighbors on either side of the home. If a neighbor, separated from you only by a twelve-inch wall, is slovenly and acquires rats and cockroaches, you'll have them to contend with too. A neighbor with a leaking roof may give you a cellar full of water. In a house of this sort, make sure of your legal rights and of the liabilities of your abutting neighbors.

We shall accept the premise that a sound savings-investment program should, if possible, include the ownership of a home. If it cannot, it does not mean necessarily that the savings-investment program without home-ownership is unsound or unworkable. It's just that by owning a home one finds it less painful, easier, to save. Ownership of a home makes for *forced* savings.

There is, for instance, the theory that, exclusive of the taxes you pay, you're living "rent-free" in your own home. In a way, you are. But you'll get your rent back from the bank or from your property only when you *sell* your home.

Until then, your home is an asset, countable in figuring your net worth. But it's a frozen asset and remains such until sold. Then, the only *real asset* insofar as you, the saver-investor, are concerned, is how much money you have left over after providing for *another* home. After all, you have to have someplace to live.

So, for the purposes of regarding a home as an investment, it is necessary to think of ways to increase the value of your home through your years of occupancy.

If you have bought carefully and wisely, your home has had an automatic appreciation in value. It's in a "protected" community where industrial and commercial growth has not harmed but has, in fact, enhanced the property values. It is in the path of the population-migration trend so that it has become more desirable to more people. You have kept it in good repair.

Meantime, what can you do to improve the value of your investment?

You can do two things: *1.* You can improve your community; and *2.* You can increase the capital value of your house.

You can participate in community affairs, social and civic. You can devote some energy to seeing that the cultural aspects of your community are enviable, that the churches, schools, parks, playgrounds, and community centers are supported and kept up. You can devote some energy to civic duties, to see that zoning laws are enacted or enforced; to see that the community's physical plan of streets, fire and police stations, and such, are in good shape; to see, additionally, that no slum areas develop or spread. You can help to keep the taxes "reasonable" —a word of much latitude—so that the tax burden won't drive away prospective property buyers.

You can add to the value of your house in numerous ways. If it's kept in good repair, if the neighborhood is a good one, if all your neighboring homes are kept up and improved, you should have property of relatively stable value through the years.

You might add a porch or a patio. You may need additional bedroom space, or more bathrooms. You might finish the cellar, make a playroom or a workshop. You may build a summer house or a swimming pool. You may landscape your lawns.

These are capital improvements. You must not count on getting all of your money back on them when you sell your home, for you won't. You can charge some of it off to pleasure, convenience, or better living.

Some capital improvements can be wasteful, however. It is silly to build an expensive swimming pool beside a home which is in a development of numerous other homes, all in the same price class and which resemble one another.

A porch or patio, however, would be a good investment in

these circumstances. On a good patio, for instance, costing, say $2000, you might expect to get $1000 more on the sale of your house.

New home owners spend a great deal of money on plants and shrubs and lawns, believing that they are increasing the worth of their property. They are not. The unfortunate aspect of it is, however, that unless they do spend quite a bit of money on such things as foundation planting and good grass seed, they'll detract from the value of their property.

A buyer expects that a brand-new home won't have much in the way of plants, shrubs, or lawns. However, when he gets a secondhand house he expects to find these things—*but he doesn't expect to pay for them.* Usually he doesn't have to.

Unless there's a very costly professional landscape job done, you can't count much on getting back any of the money you invested in the lawn or outside property. However, good fences or good boundary plants *are* of value in reselling a house.

It's safest to keep in mind what you'd be willing to pay for if *you* were buying your house again.

Thus, you are saving some cash.

You are saving through the purchase of your home.

In a way, you have already begun to invest. The cash you are saving is being invested by the bank and you're getting some interest on your money.

Your investment in your home is being nurtured and cultivated.

You are getting ready for the time when you can invest your cash directly, handle the investment yourself, and get the full yield.

Your home is a reserve of cash, waiting for your ultimate retirement, when you'll want to sell it, take the money you've saved, and go on with the fulfillment of this program of *Save It, Invest It, and Retire.*

Generally speaking, real estate is a good investment. More often than not it's a safe investment.

Thus far in the savings program I have recommended savings in cash and savings in real estate. This is advised because of the soundness of this economic principle: *In economic fluctuations, real estate and cash savings will be on opposite sides of the movement.*

For example, when there's inflation, the value of the dollars saved in *cash* depreciates. Cash is worth less because it buys less. But at the same time the value of real estate will be higher.

Conversely, in times of depression, the value of saved *cash* increases even though the value of real estate decreases.

By saving both in cash and in real estate, you have hedged your investments against the rises and falls in the economic chart lines. It's the simplest, yet safest hedge there is. Still, it's the one least employed and least advised by the "experts"; perhaps because it's too uncomplicated.

Real estate is such an attractive investment that many may find it useful in expanding their real estate holdings into something besides a home.

For instance, the person who buys a combination business-residential property such as one sees in the residential periphery of all cities, has bought not only a home but a source of rental income as well. If, as a structure and as a combination building, it measures up to all the rules in the previous chapter that would apply to it, then it is a sound investment indeed.

The owner of such a building can feel more comfortable about his real estate and his financial affairs. Should anything happen to him, his widow would be assured not only of a home but of a supplemental income from the rents.

I know of just such a situation, except the husband did not arrange for it. The widow took his insurance money and shopped around until she found just what she wanted. She paid $30,000 for a building that had two small stores—a stationery-soda shop and a delicatessen—and two upstairs apartments, one of six rooms and the top floor of five rooms.

The building needed about $5000 worth of repairs. She paid

cash for it, had the repairs made, and figured her total investment at about $35,000.

With her family grown and her husband dead she no longer needed the large ten-room home she had been living in, so she sold it for $48,000, paid off the $5000 mortgage that remained, and put the rest into savings and investments.

Then she moved into the five-room flat on the top floor, rented the six-room flat for $200 a month, and kept the same rents on the two stores that the previous owner had asked, $275 for the delicatessen and $200 for the stationery-soda shop.

So she has her rent paid and a gross income of $675 a month, $8100 a year. She pays about $2000 for taxes and insurance and save out about $1500 a year for upkeep of the property. That leaves her net income of $4600. That's more than $80 a week. Where else can you invest $35,000 and get $4600 per year return —over 13 per cent? And your rent thrown in for free!

Sometimes it's a good investment to buy a house, solely for the purpose of renting it to others. On good property, in a favorable location, net rental income will yield between 10 and 15 per cent of invested capital.

I know of a young couple who were comfortably set up in their own home, living on a decent income and faithfully engaged in a savings program when they discovered in their community a fine, inexpensive house for sale for $20,000. They investigated and learned that to buy it they'd need $4000 cash for a down payment and would have to pay about $100 monthly for twenty years on a mortgage. Further investigation showed that on the basis of rents in the area, they could expect to charge $180 a month rent, and that there would probably be customers at that price.

They bought it. They may or may not have been wise. It's rather complicated figuring, but here's how it works out:

He pays the bank $101 a month, or $1212 a year.
He receives in rent $180 a month, or $2560 a year.
That means he has a *net from rents* of $1348 a year.

But of the $101 per month which he pays the bank, $25 a month goes directly to amortize his mortgage and the remainder goes to pay taxes, water, insurance, interest, and maintain the escrow account. So he says he's in reality *saving* $25 a month or $300 per year with his mortgage payments.

Thus, adding the $300 to the $1348 net from rents, he figures his combined savings and income from the property is $1648.

As his mortgage is paid down and there is less principal on which interest is charged, his monthly "savings" in the equity of the property will increase. In fact it increases slightly each month. He regards this as "savings," which, indeed, it is—actually it's "forced savings." Over the 20 year period, if rentals were to remain the same, his income from rents would be $26,960, which would be much greater than the cost of the mortgage. Of course, some of his "profit" would have to go to upkeep of the property.

However, if property values increase during the next 20 years as they have in the last two decades, his $20,000 house should be worth $35,000 or more by the time he has paid off the mortgage and owns it free and clear.

The least one can say of this young man is that he has courage. I'm not sure I'd like to participate in such a program, but I'd bet a week's pay that he succeeds in his plan. He has not counted on upkeep costs for the property, but he's a do-it-yourself fan with a well-equipped basement workshop. With a more subjective appraisal of the scheme, it's probably just an extension of his hobby—a rather inexpensive extension to the hobby, and one which one day will have a payoff.

It's interesting to note that he and his wife refer to this as their "retirement investment."

Another form of real estate investment that has always interested me is the purchases of sites for speculation, sites with a potential for business location and sites that might someday be in the path of housing development.

This requires a fairly intimate knowledge of locale, but it is frequently a rewarding effort to study an area and hazard a few speculative dollars on the ownership of a vacant lot.

The small investor with a serious yen to put his money into real estate can raise his sights a bit, these days, and through the function of real estate syndicates, can buy into large office buildings, apartment houses, and industrial plants. Previously the syndicates functioned for the invested dollars of the well-to-do, but in the past year or so there has sprung up a market for investors with small nest eggs.

The fact is, as noted heretofore, good real estate investments can be made with comparative safety. The yield on investment can be 10-to-15 per cent and even higher, compared to the yield on good blue-chip securities of 6-to-8 per cent. The advent of the "syndicate" now makes it possible to enter the real estate investment field with relatively small amounts of capital and relatively small margin.

It stands to reason. A mortgage equal to 60 per cent of the value of the property means that the title owner or owners operate with a margin of only 40 per cent. Much higher ratios are not uncommon, particularly when syndicates of several buyers are involved. Moreover, in such cases, second mortgages are frequently taken out to ease the burden of financing.

The feature of "margin" has its interesting aspects to the small investor. A mortgage note—the borrowed funds—will not be callable until the specified date of the mortgage, no matter how many years are involved. On the other hand, the investor in stocks and securities who employs margin might find, with a sudden dip in the market, that he is forced to put up more money to cover his stocks.

The one thing to remember, however, is that real estate is not a "liquid asset." It can't be converted into cash easily or quickly, particularly in times of recession. It's not a question of calling up a broker and asking him to sell, as with the owner of stocks.

The large real estate syndicates operate something like the specialized mutual funds on the stock exchanges. They spread their ownership over several real estate enterprises in the expectation of lessening any peril.

Syndicates for buying large buildings or big tracts are formed by professional real estate investors or sometimes by brokers who hear of good deals coming along.

In New York and Chicago there are probably hundreds of small, profitable syndicates, formed among friends, which function smoothly, bringing fine income to the members. This method of investment is having growing popularity in other cities as well.

When a broker or a professional real estate investor hears of a large property which can be bought for, say, $500,000 over the existing mortgage, he calls five potential syndicate investors and asks them for $100,000 each, or ten investors for $50,000 each, or twenty investors and asks for $25,000 each, and so on.

Anyone interested in this kind of investment can be put in touch with a broker specializing in this kind of property and this type of deal by consulting his local real estate board or even his neighborhood real estate broker.

The investor in a syndicate should remember he's entering a legal partnership and investments of this nature are two-way streets. While they provide larger-than-usual yields in income, they also carry larger-than-normal legal responsibilities. The venture should be guided with a competent lawyer and the property should be appraised by an expert.

In this examination of real estate investments, I have assiduously avoided dealing with farms and farmland, for it is my belief that no one should buy a farm without an exhaustive knowledge of the subject. Farms are not merely homes or investment properties. They're businesses. As much technical knowledge is required—should be required—as is expected of the manufacturer who seeks an industrial site.

There are so many factors—soil, climate, access to markets, condition of connecting roads and highways, water supply and-/or rainfall record, condition and efficiency of buildings, histories of crop experiences, and such—that the prospective purchaser of farm property should proceed only under expert guidance.

The section on retirement, however, will deal at greater length on some aspects of farming suited to the semiretired person or the horticultural hobbyist.

Chapter 4

Saving with Insurance

THE FIRST AND MOST IMPORTANT STEP IN ANY SAVINGS PLAN IS A program of life insurance. It's a necessity—almost as necessary as having a job or an income. Yet the experts of family finance and personal finance are amazed each year when the Institute of Life Insurance issues its annual figures of life insurance ownership revealing how few persons actually own insurance and, among those who own it, how little they possess. A late report shows that out of 205,000,000 Americans only 140,000,000 owned life insurance.

These round figures are deceptive, of course, for this includes the $500 and $1000 policies taken out by proud fathers on their youngsters. It makes the total ownership larger and reduces the average size of the policy holdings. Insured families own an average of $21,800 worth of life insurance, according to the Institute of Life Insurance.

Yet no student of family finance will disagree when it is stated categorically that most Americans do not own enough life insurance, that a majority do not sufficiently avail themselves of this cheapest and easiest form of savings.

The blame, however, belongs with the life insurance companies. They have not spread their message to the people, and the message that has been put across is misleading and often uninformative.

One large company has for years advertised nothing but health information, a noble cause, particularly in view of the achievements in reducing disease incidence and raising the life expectancy levels during the past couple of decades. But this hardly serves the industry which has made this company one of the wealthiest corporations in the world. Another company has featured a campaign for a long span of years, plugging retirement insurance, again a splendid cause, but one which fails by a wide margin to tell the insurance story.

I charge that a great many of those who now own life insurance have insurance programs they don't need or programs they don't want. They are reluctant owners, holding their policies because of the fear of death and the knowledge that their widows and families need the protection, and a vague realization of the fact that sound personal finance calls for the ownership of some kind of insurance.

I further submit that a great many of the insurance owners of the nation have only a skimpy knowledge of what they own or what their policy guarantees or does not guarantee, and that most of those who have bought insurance did not, at the time of purchase, get to look over all the merchandise, study the other plans and programs available, and make a *selective* decision on the policy they wanted.

I'll wager:

> That less than 5 per cent of those who own life insurance shopped around to see if other companies offered better plans.
> That less than 50 per cent of those who own life insurance asked their insurance salesman about other plans offered by his company.

This is not the fault of the salesmen. It's the fault of the companies.

The companies have gone to great pains to devise numerous flexible insurance programs designed to fit a wide variety of needs and circumstances. At the top level they have exhibited professional qualities of the first rank. But as a whole they have ignored the primary fact that they are in a service industry and that their services must be *sold.* Not that the companies aren't sales-conscious. Perhaps they're too sales-conscious, at the expense of acceptability, promotion, or that immensely valuable, yet so elusive factor, "good will," or believability.

In the eyes of the public the man who sells insurance is in the same category as any other door-to-door salesman, just like the fellow who sells magazines or brushes or storm windows. He is not regarded as a professional man, armed with specialized knowledge which might be specially useful to a person with but scant knowledge in the field of personal finance.

Yet that's what the insurance salesman should be—a professional man, a counselor, adviser, family-budget planner, as smoothly competent, as highly ethical as a man of medicine.

Insurance salesmen have recognized this and with their professional organizations have sought to raise the professional standards of their numbers. But qualification comes at the culmination of a long, tough grind. Meanwhile insurance salesmen, like others, must feed and clothe their families. And they soon find that most companies don't much care about the particular qualifications of an individual salesman, so long as the sales records stay intact.

Admittedly it's hard to find good insurance salesmen. The hours are long and the selling is tough. Most sales are made at night when the breadwinners are home from work, and collections are made by day when the housewives fret at the interruption. I do not presume to know the solution to the problem. But if the insurance companies accept as a challenge the fact that so few Americans own insurance, then they must think about improving the professional quality of their salesmanship.

The fact is, now they're selling policies, where they should be selling the theory of insurance. The salesmen are persuading customers to "spend" a few dollars for coverage, where they should be counseling customers on the methods of accumulating savings, benefits, estates, and security.

The range of life insurance programs is broad. A smart shopper in life insurance can pick up almost any kind of tailor-made budget-fitting program to meet individual needs.

The greatest single mistake generally made about insurance is the belief that you "buy it." Indeed, insurance people themselves spread this concept by asking if they can "sell it" to you.

You don't *buy insurance; you save it.*

For most purposes it is unwise to regard insurance for the death benefits provided by it; rather to consider it as a flexible form of savings which provides the added bonus of automatically creating an estate for the survivors of the insured. But until the insured dies, it isn't insurance at all; it's a savings account—a form of investment even.

In its original concept, life insurance was, in fact, nothing more than a guaranteed death benefit, a cooperative risk-sharing, with the insurance company betting a specified amount of money on the individual. Over the years the companies worked out "actuarially" the basic percentages of life expectancy so that it is possible to know just about how many of the thirty-year-old men who buy life insurance this week will still be alive twenty years from now or thirty years from now. This, in turn, makes it possible to determine just how much should be charged to permit the insurance companies to remain in business.

Throughout the years, however, the original theme has been elaborated upon as the demands of informed savers were intensified so that today there are myriad plans enabling people to set aside portions of their income during their working-and-earning years to provide for the time when their incomes are cut off, not only by death, but by retirement or illness in the declining years. It is possible to build a nearly complete program of savings-and-investment around a few insurance policies.

The study of this theory on how to save, invest, and retire is predicated on the assumption that in these days most people will find it impossible either to retain enough of what they earn or save enough of what they retain to provide for the uncertainties of life. Insurance plans are designed to overcome some part of this modern problem.

Insurance, in its pure form, is a cooperative financial stunt. When an individual buys a policy he is, in effect, getting a membership card in a group which is sharing all risks and which promises to pay to the person or persons selected by him, a specified sum upon his death. This promise is made in return for a promise from the policyholder that he will pay a stated sum of money at regular intervals—weekly, monthly, quarterly, or annually—either for the balance of his life or for a specified period at which time his membership in the group will be "paid up."

There are minimum requirements. He must be in sound health, else the unhealthy would buy the most insurance and the healthy would postpone their participation with the result that the cost would be prohibitive or the "group" (company) could not survive. For the same reasons he cannot work in a hazardous job without paying a higher premium.

But if he can pass a physical examination and if his occupation is satisfactory and acceptable to the company, he can participate in the risk-sharing and his survivors or beneficiaries can be assured of a specified sum of money at a specified time.

Note well: *You do not have to die in order to get your money out of insurance.*

A policyholder can benefit equally as much as his beneficiaries if he will make the effort to learn all that his policy can do for him.

A policy may promise to pay a lump sum of money to a beneficiary at the time of death of the insured. That's what most policies provide. Or it might be an endowment policy and promise to pay the money to the insured at a certain time if he still lives at the time it matures.

Nearly all policies these days give the buyer a choice of leaving a lump sum to his survivor or having the beneficiary receive the money in monthly allotments, like income. The insurance companies have figured it out actuarially so that they can tell you just what your beneficiary will receive if you order one of five good plans:

1. A monthly income for life.

2. Monthly payments for a specified length of time, with interest added.

3. Equal monthly payments of such an amount that the life insurance money, with its interest, is used up in a specified period of time.

4. Leave the money "on deposit" with the company, where it will draw interest until it is needed by the beneficiary.

5. Leave the decision with the beneficiary, who may ask for the money in lump sum, or monthly, or who may prefer to let it remain with the insurance company and collect interest.

The cheapest kind of life insurance is called "term" insurance; it's also probably the most impractical. It serves only one purpose: to insure the life of the person named in the policy. It is good only as long as the payments are kept up and is cancellable as soon as a payment is missed. There are no accumulated benefits, there is no loan value, there is no cash-surrender value.

Every serviceman of World War II and after has been exposed to term insurance—GI insurance. When on active service the GIs had term insurance, paid monthly by deductions from service pay. After a GI was discharged it was possible to continue this as term insurance, convert it to ten-, twenty- or thirty-payment life insurance (meaning the policy is paid up in ten, twenty, or thirty years) or whole life—meaning it will never be "paid up," that the policyholder will have to continue paying monthly premiums until he dies, although as time goes on he will have "paid-up" options and definite cash-surrender value or loan value.

Thus term insurance provides only temporary protection. It insures a person for a specified "term" of time, say, five years. If he does not die within that time, he has lost all that he has put into the insurance.

That is not true of other kinds of policies.

What, then, is the value of term insurance? It provides the maximum protection for the minimum cost. That's why the government uses it for its servicemen. It's useful protection on a father's life while his children are growing, particularly in these days of increasing heart attacks, for it permits him at minimum cost to have more insurance coverage than he could normally afford.

Proceeding up the ladder in cost, the next least expensive insurance is whole life. It's the most useful, flexible, practical insurance anyone can buy. It's the kind I own and the kind I might recommend as a counselor on family finance.

You don't have to die to get the benefits of a whole-life policy. Yet if you do, your beneficiaries get full payment. It provides savings, investment (because the companies pay interest on your money), security, and even—if you handle it right—your own private built-in retirement plan.

Presumably, when one embarks on a whole-life policy program, he agrees to make regular payments of premiums until he dies. But usually in twenty or thirty years, or at least by the age of sixty-five, there is enough cash value to the policy to provide for paid-up insurance, if not for the full face value of the policy, then certainly for a policy of a little less value. After all, at sixty-five, does one have to leave as much money to his wife and children as he would have had to leave at, say, forty-five years of age, when the wife faced many more years of possible widowhood and the children were much younger, perhaps not through with their schooling?

If at the age of sixty-five a person is ready to retire, he doesn't *need* so much life insurance. His children are grown, his home is paid for, his savings program is complete, his investments are in good shape. There's social security coming in and he and his wife can look forward to only ten or fifteen "good" years. Why should he carry a "heavy" insurance load?

That's where the versatility of a whole-life policy is advantageous. It can be adapted to changing needs. The sixty-five-year-old man of the preceding paragraph could take a fully paid-up policy. Or he could arrange for a guaranteed annuity for himself, or a guaranteed annuity for himself and his wife, paid jointly and to survivor.

Technically these privileges are known as "nonforfeiture values." They're listed in every whole-life policy. They permit the policyholder to borrow money from his life insurance, using the policy as collateral. Or he can stop paying his premiums, yet be protected with insurance on a modified scale. Or he can take a cash settlement—either the full value or part of the value. Or he can combine all of these things. *He gets back the money he has put into his policy* minus the cost of insuring him through the years.

For the average family I recommend whole-life insurance, programed this way:

1. Buy just as much insurance as you can possibly afford while you are young and have dependents.

2. When this protection is no longer needed and retirement is in sight, (*a*) stop paying premiums; (*b*) take a portion of the cash-surrender value of the policy in cash or as guaranteed annual income (depending on whether cash is needed to help accomplish the retirement, such as buying a small, part-time business); and (*c*) leave the remainder as paid-up insurance.

In effect, the head of the household is still insured—but for a reduced amount. He has traded, at age sixty-five, his death benefits for an income or cash.

Consider the young man of thirty-two who decides he can afford $20,000 worth of life insurance which, at that age, would cost him about $450 a year in a mutual company. (Many of the large companies are mutual companies, as opposed to stock companies which are owned by the investors who have bought shares in the companies.) He's going to buy this at a cost of, say, $40 a month.

This includes, incidentally, $2.00 a month for double indemnity—the accidental-death benefit—which means that if he is killed by natural causes such as in an automobile accident or in a fall off a ladder or some such mishap, his beneficiary would receive twice the amount of the policy, or $40,000. Since the young man is of good health, he figures his death, if it comes at all, will be precipitated by violent means, thus the double indemnity coverage is worth-while.

At the age of sixty-two, he will have paid on his policy for thirty years. He'll have paid $450 a year, or, in thirty years, $13,500.

That's all he has paid, yet for thirty years he has been insured for $20,000 in the event he died of illness or disease and $40,000 in the event of a violent end.

But this young man survived, so he gave the company $13,500 over a period of thirty years. Now, at age sixty-two, he finds that he owns:

A policy which has cash surrender and loan values of $9560.

Paid-up life insurance worth $13,560 if he doesn't pay another dime in premiums—actually $60 more than he has put in!

Term insurance worth $20,000, extended and guaranteed by the company for the next sixteen years, two hundred and nineteen days, or until he reaches nearly seventy-nine years of age.

The policyholder, no longer young, but still hale, decides to wait until he's sixty-five before retiring, for then he will get some Social Security benefits to help him along.

Three years later, on his sixty-fifth birthday, he takes his policy out to check his accumulated wealth.

He has a policy worth $11,300 in cash surrender and loan values.

He has paid-up life insurance of $15,000.

He has paid-up term insurance worth $20,000 for the next

fifteen years, nineteen days—or until he's a little over eighty years old.

This fellow has had his eye on a variety store in Florida for several years. He knows he can buy it. He needs some cash.

Now its safe to assume that a man with such a well-managed life up to this point has the necessary cash in savings and convertible securities or tied up in the house he's going to sell before he moves to Florida. But on the supposition that he doesn't have it, he could elect to take half of the cash-surrender value.

It's figured that he can get $565 in cash for each $1000 of the face value of the policy. He's going to take half of his $20,000 policy, or $10,000 worth of cash-surrender value. It comes out to $5650.

The company figures he has paid-up insurance calculated at $750 for each $1000 of face value of the policy. He has $10,000 worth of "face value" left, as he converts this to paid-up life insurance. That gives him $7500 worth of paid-up life insurance on which he doesn't have to spend another cent. It's probably more than will be needed, but he likes to know that there is that much available for contingencies.

He has $5650 in cash and $7500 in paid-up insurance.

Added together that's a total of $13,150.

Yet, over thirty-three years he has paid the company only $14,850.

Subtract the $13,150 from the $14,850 and it can be seen that he has paid only $1700 for $20,000 worth of life insurance for thirty-three years. The rest of it is *savings.*

If there's a better bargain than that anywhere under the sun, it'll be a great deal harder to find than an insurance agent who would write a policy like the one described in the foregoing.

This is the most popular kind of insurance, the easiest to buy, the least expensive in the long run, and the kind I recommend as being particularly adapted to the program set forth in this study.

Of course, a great deal depends on the individual plans. For good reasons some may not want to commit themselves to a lifetime of paying premiums. They may want to concentrate this responsibility in their most productive years.

They can get a limited-payment life policy which, like the whole-life policy, provides lifetime protection. Yet, it limits the payment of premiums for any period the insured may desire, such as ten, twenty, or thirty years. It has limits on the other end, too, so that the policy is paid up at a certain age, say sixty, sixty-five, or seventy. If the time for paying premiums is limited, then the premium rate is higher. But the cash values are higher, too, than are those in a whole-life policy. In all other respects the two policies are similar.

A man who has established a successful business career at the age of thirty-five can take out a thirty-year limited-payment life policy and plan to retire at the age of sixty-five. At the magic age of sixty-five his policy is paid in full and he can either gather up his cash and go fishing or elect to have a lifetime income from the proceeds. Meanwhile, during the intervening thirty years, he has had full insurance coverage on his life.

In insurance, more than in anything else, *you get what you pay for.*

Anyone who works out a plan of his own, permitting him to make the most of his productive years so that he can provide for a snug and happy retirement, can find, with a little inquiry, an insurance program that will seem virtually custom-made to individual requirements.

There are many other kinds of insurance which will be discussed briefly in an appendage to this chapter. For most purposes, however, the two forms outlined in detail herein, whole-life and limited-payment life, are the best insurance policies for the average fellow with average income and normal prospects.

Stop thinking of it as "life" insurance. It's "savings" insurance. Rather, it starts out as *life* insurance and ends up as *savings* insurance, if all goes as planned.

Insurance should be viewed *and* handled in perspective. A young couple in their twenties or thirties should be buying "life" insurance. The husband should be insured for as much as he can possibly afford.

You'll note here that I advise excesses in all parts of this program: save all you can afford; buy as much of a home as you can possibly afford; buy the maximum amount of insurance that you can afford.

Why should the young couple insure the husband's life excessively? Common sense holds the answer. If he should die at the age of thirty or thirty-five, his widow will face forty years or more of solitary responsibility and she may have growing children in her care and a home to pay for and maintain.

At this time of life it's *life* insurance. Regard it in its proper perspective: *you have to die to win all the money.* If that unfortunate event does occur, it's a good thing to have so much insurance.

On the other hand, would a woman who becomes a widow at sixty or sixty-five or seventy need so much insurance? The children have grown and left, the home should be paid for, Social Security is imminent or already being paid, the needs are less and the expensive tastes have been satisfied long since.

The young man who started with an excessive and expensive *life* insurance program twenty-five or thirty years earlier now finds he has *savings* insurance.

Now he is in a position to *win* even though he didn't die. Most of the money he has saved in life insurance is available to him in cash, in guaranteed income, or as money left on deposit with the insurance company.

This, then, is what I recommend: Buy as much life insurance as you can afford. Don't begrudge its periodic demands for your money—it's *your* money and will be available either to your beneficiary or ultimately to yourself. Then, when the time comes to retire, *use* your insurance money, leaving enough in a paid-up policy to care for final expenses and provide a bit of ready cash for your widow.

In an earlier book of mine, *Teach Your Wife to Be a Widow,*
I advocated having insurance paid to a widow in a lump sum,
after teaching her how to invest the money, on the grounds that
she could make a great deal more money by investing it wisely
than she would get by drawing monthly allotments from the
insurance company. For this advice I was taken to task by some
insurance companies and insurance associations because, they
said, a widow would lose all the money in Wall Street and all
that saving and stinting through the years would have been
wasted. These critics ignored completely the fact that I had
advocated *first* that a woman be instructed in the craftsman-
ship of stock market investment.

This is an illogical criticism, anyway, because the insurance
companies, if they retain the benefits and do not pay out the
money in lump sum, do just exactly what I had advocated—
they invest the money in securities, bonds, and mortgages.
Some insurance companies have even underwritten some em-
barrassing projects and found themselves owning ungainly
white elephants.

At any rate, under the section on retirement, I shall again
advocate investing some part of the insurance money after taking the cash-surrender value of a major portion of the money
that has been accumulated in *savings* insurance. This is not for
a helpless widow but for a man and wife who, if they have
followed this program, have learned how to invest money
wisely and profitably.

I cannot stress too strongly the need for a full, a *maximum*
life insurance program.

Do not get talked into making an insurance program a substi-
tute for a savings program, however. Insurance *becomes* savings in time; it is *not* savings while it's being built up.

Cash savings are necessary in this over-all plan. Cash is always available.

The savings in real estate are not readily available.

The savings in insurance, while available, are not very easy
to get at and moreover, in order to keep a policy in force, you

cannot *withdraw* the cash you have accumulated through insurance, you have to *borrow* it. The insurance companies charge you interest to let you borrow your own money. This is one bad feature of insurance and one which companies have tried to remove for many years. Unfortunately it's necessary, for if your policy guarantees that your beneficiary will receive a stipulated amount in the event of your death, the company needs the use of your money all the time, so it can be earning enough—through investments—to pay that benefit in case it's required. Thus, if you need the money, you have to pay interest on it. In that way it becomes an "investment" to the company; it's out earning its keep.

At the end of the chapter you will find tables of loan and nonforfeiture values, both for whole-life and for limited-payment life insurance programs. From them you will be able to determine just how many years it will take you to accumulate the *savings* insurance you need. The figures are calculated for each $1000 of insurance. Thus, if you own $30,000 worth of insurance, multiply the figure by thirty.

It would be impossible to print in this volume all of the actuarial tables to enable each individual to determine how much insurance would cost him. Here's a rough idea, though:

Suppose you are thirty-five years old and want to purchase $25,000 worth of insurance.

A twenty-year endowment would cost you about $1313 a year.

A twenty-payment life policy would cost about $1020 a year.

A thirty-year endowment would cost about $893 a year.

A thirty-payment life policy would cost about $791 a year.

Whole-life (ordinary life) would cost about $714 a year.

Ten-year renewable term would cost about $281 a year.

Five-year renewable term would cost about $255 a year.

MONTHLY INCOME FOR EACH $1,000 OF PROCEEDS

(This Option is available only for endowment or surrender proceeds, if any)

The income will be based on the ages (at nearest birthday on the due date of the first income payment) of the 2 persons during whose joint lifetime payments are to be made, and will be reduced to two thirds after the first death.

AGE OF MALE

AGE OF FEMALE	55	56	57	58	59	60	61	62	63	64	65	66	67	68	69	70	71	72	73	74	75
50	$4.04	4.08	4.12	4.16	4.19	4.23	4.27	4.31	4.35	4.39	4.43	4.47	4.51	4.56	4.60	4.64	4.68	4.72	4.76	4.80	4.84
51	4.10	4.13	4.17	4.21	4.25	4.29	4.33	4.38	4.42	4.46	4.50	4.54	4.59	4.63	4.67	4.72	4.76	4.80	4.85	4.89	4.93
52	4.15	4.19	4.23	4.27	4.31	4.36	4.40	4.44	4.48	4.53	4.57	4.62	4.66	4.71	4.75	4.80	4.84	4.89	4.93	4.98	5.02
53	4.20	4.25	4.29	4.33	4.38	4.42	4.46	4.51	4.55	4.60	4.65	4.69	4.74	4.79	4.83	4.88	4.93	4.97	5.02	5.07	5.11
54	4.26	4.30	4.35	4.40	4.44	4.49	4.53	4.58	4.63	4.68	4.72	4.77	4.82	4.87	4.92	4.97	5.02	5.07	5.12	5.16	5.21
55	4.32	4.37	4.41	4.46	4.51	4.56	4.60	4.65	4.70	4.75	4.80	4.85	4.91	4.96	5.01	5.06	5.11	5.16	5.21	5.26	5.32
56	4.38	4.43	4.48	4.53	4.58	4.63	4.68	4.73	4.78	4.83	4.89	4.94	4.99	5.05	5.10	5.16	5.21	5.26	5.32	5.37	5.42
57	4.44	4.49	4.54	4.59	4.65	4.70	4.75	4.81	4.86	4.92	4.97	5.03	5.08	5.14	5.20	5.26	5.31	5.37	5.42	5.48	5.54
58	4.50	4.55	4.61	4.66	4.72	4.77	4.83	4.89	4.95	5.00	5.06	5.12	5.18	5.24	5.30	5.36	5.42	5.48	5.54	5.60	5.66
59	4.56	4.62	4.68	4.73	4.79	4.85	4.91	4.97	5.03	5.09	5.15	5.22	5.28	5.34	5.40	5.47	5.53	5.59	5.66	5.72	5.78
60	4.63	4.69	4.75	4.81	4.87	4.93	4.99	5.06	5.12	5.18	5.25	5.32	5.38	5.45	5.51	5.58	5.65	5.71	5.78	5.85	5.91
61	4.69	4.76	4.82	4.88	4.95	5.01	5.08	5.14	5.21	5.28	5.35	5.42	5.49	5.56	5.63	5.70	5.77	5.84	5.91	5.98	6.05
62	4.76	4.83	4.89	4.96	5.03	5.09	5.16	5.23	5.31	5.38	5.45	5.52	5.60	5.67	5.75	5.82	5.90	5.97	6.05	6.12	6.19
63	4.83	4.90	4.97	5.04	5.11	5.18	5.25	5.33	5.40	5.48	5.55	5.63	5.71	5.79	5.87	5.95	6.03	6.11	6.19	6.26	6.34
64	4.90	4.97	5.04	5.12	5.19	5.27	5.34	5.42	5.50	5.58	5.66	5.74	5.83	5.91	6.00	6.08	6.16	6.25	6.33	6.42	6.50
65	4.97	5.04	5.12	5.20	5.27	5.35	5.44	5.52	5.60	5.69	5.77	5.86	5.95	6.04	6.13	6.22	6.31	6.40	6.49	6.58	6.66
66	5.04	5.12	5.20	5.28	5.36	5.44	5.53	5.62	5.71	5.80	5.89	5.98	6.07	6.17	6.26	6.36	6.45	6.55	6.65	6.74	6.84
67	5.11	5.19	5.28	5.36	5.45	5.54	5.62	5.72	5.81	5.91	6.00	6.10	6.20	6.30	6.40	6.50	6.61	6.71	6.81	6.91	7.02
68	5.18	5.27	5.35	5.44	5.53	5.63	5.72	5.82	5.92	6.02	6.12	6.22	6.33	6.44	6.55	6.65	6.76	6.87	6.98	7.09	7.20
69	5.26	5.34	5.44	5.53	5.62	5.72	5.82	5.92	6.03	6.13	6.24	6.35	6.46	6.58	6.69	6.81	6.93	7.04	7.16	7.28	7.40
70	5.33	5.42	5.52	5.61	5.71	5.82	5.92	6.03	6.14	6.25	6.37	6.48	6.60	6.72	6.84	6.97	7.09	7.22	7.34	7.47	7.60
71	5.40	5.50	5.60	5.70	5.80	5.91	6.02	6.13	6.25	6.37	6.49	6.61	6.74	6.87	7.00	7.13	7.26	7.40	7.53	7.67	7.81
72	5.48	5.58	5.68	5.78	5.89	6.00	6.12	6.24	6.36	6.49	6.62	6.75	6.88	7.02	7.16	7.30	7.44	7.58	7.73	7.87	8.02
73	5.55	5.65	5.76	5.87	5.98	6.10	6.22	6.35	6.48	6.61	6.74	6.88	7.02	7.17	7.32	7.47	7.62	7.77	7.93	8.09	8.24
74	5.62	5.73	5.84	5.96	6.08	6.20	6.32	6.45	6.59	6.73	6.87	7.02	7.17	7.32	7.48	7.64	7.80	7.97	8.13	8.30	8.47
75	5.70	5.81	5.92	6.04	6.17	6.29	6.43	6.56	6.70	6.85	7.00	7.15	7.31	7.47	7.64	7.81	7.99	8.17	8.34	8.53	8.71

The income for any other combination of ages or for 2 persons of the same sex will be quoted upon request.

MONTHLY INCOME FOR EACH $1,000 OF PROCEEDS
The life income will be based on the payee's age at nearest
birthday on the due date of the first income payment.

			MALE PAYEE			
AGE	10 Yrs. Certain	20 Yrs. Certain	Refund Period Certain	AGE	10 Yrs. Certain	20 Yrs. Certain	Refund Period Certain
*10	$2.49	$2.48	$2.47	46	$3.93	$3.77	$3.70
11	2.50	2.50	2.49	47	4.01	3.83	3.77
12	2.52	2.52	2.50	48	4.10	3.89	3.84
13	2.54	2.54	2.52	49	4.18	3.95	3.90
14	2.56	2.56	2.54				
				50	4.28	4.01	3.98
15	2.58	2.58	2.56	51	4.37	4.08	4.05
16	2.60	2.60	2.58	52	4.47	4.14	4.13
17	2.63	2.62	2.60	53	4.57	4.20	4.22
18	2.65	2.64	2.62	54	4.68	4.27	4.30
19	2.67	2.67	2.65				
				55	4.79	4.33	4.39
20	2.70	2.69	2.67	56	4.91	4.40	4.49
21	2.73	2.72	2.69	57	5.03	4.46	4.59
22	2.75	2.74	2.72	58	5.15	4.52	4.69
23	2.78	2.77	2.75	59	5.29	4.59	4.80
24	2.81	2.80	2.77				
				60	5.42	4.65	4.91
25	2.84	2.83	2.80	61	5.57	4.70	5.04
26	2.87	2.86	2.83	62	5.71	4.76	5.16
27	2.91	2.89	2.86	63	5.87	4.81	5.30
28	2.94	2.93	2.89	64	6.03	4.86	5.44
29	2.98	2.96	2.92				
				65	6.19	4.90	5.59
30	3.02	3.00	2.96	66	6.36	4.95	5.74
31	3.06	3.03	2.99	67	6.54	4.98	5.91
32	3.10	3.07	3.03	68	6.71	5.02	6.09
33	3.14	3.11	3.06	69	6.89	5.04	6.27
34	3.19	3.15	3.10				
				70	7.08	5.07	6.47
35	3.24	3.20	3.14	71	7.26	5.09	6.68
36	3.29	3.24	3.18	72	7.44	5.11	6.90
37	3.34	3.29	3.23	73	7.62	5.12	7.14
38	3.39	3.33	3.27	74	7.80	5.13	7.39
39	3.45	3.38	3.32				
				75	7.97	5.14	7.65
40	3.51	3.43	3.37	76	8.13	5.15	7.94
41	3.57	3.48	3.42	77	8.29	5.15	8.23
42	3.64	3.54	3.47	78	8.43	5.15	8.56
43	3.71	3.59	3.53	79	8.57	5.15	8.90
44	3.78	3.65	3.58	†80	8.69	5.16	9.26
45	3.85	3.71	3.64	*and under †and over			

MONTHLY INCOME FOR EACH $1,000 OF PROCEEDS
The life income will be based on the payee's age at nearest
birthday on the due date of the first income payment.

FEMALE PAYEE							
AGE	10 Yrs. Certain	20 Yrs. Certain	Refund Period Certain	AGE	19 Yrs. Certain	20 Yrs. Certain	Refund Period Certain
*10	$2.39	$2.39	$2.38	46	$3.53	$3.47	$3.41
11	2.40	2.40	2.39	47	3.60	3.52	3.47
12	2.42	2.42	2.41	48	3.67	3.58	3.53
13	2.44	2.43	2.42	49	3.74	3.64	3.59
14	2.45	2.45	2.44				
				50	3.81	3.70	3.65
15	2.47	2.47	2.46	51	3.89	3.76	3.71
16	2.49	2.48	2.47	52	3.97	3.83	3.78
17	2.51	2.50	2.49	53	4.06	3.90	3.86
18	2.53	2.52	2.51	54	4.15	3.97	3.93
19	2.55	2.54	2.53				
				55	4.25	4.04	4.01
20	2.57	2.56	2.55	56	4.35	4.11	4.09
21	2.59	2.58	2.57	57	4.46	4.18	4.18
22	2.61	2.60	2.59	58	4.57	4.25	4.27
23	2.63	2.63	2.61	59	4.69	4.33	4.37
24	2.66	2.65	2.63				
				60	4.82	4.40	4.47
25	2.68	2.67	2.66	61	4.95	4.47	4.58
26	2.71	2.70	2.68	62	5.09	4.54	4.70
27	2.73	2.73	2.70	63	5.23	4.61	4.82
28	2.76	2.75	2.73	64	5.39	4.68	4.94
29	2.79	2.78	2.76				
				65	5.55	4.74	5.08
30	2.82	2.81	2.78	66	5.71	4.80	5.22
31	2.85	2.84	2.81	67	5.89	4.86	5.37
32	2.89	2.87	2.84	68	6.07	4.91	5.53
33	2.92	2.90	2.87	69	6.26	4.95	5.70
34	2.96	2.94	2.91				
				70	6.45	4.99	5.88
35	2.99	2.97	2.94	71	6.65	5.03	6.07
36	3.03	3.01	2.97	72	6.85	5.06	6.27
37	3.07	3.05	3.01	73	7.05	5.08	6.49
38	3.11	3.09	3.05	74	7.26	5.10	6.72
39	3.16	3.13	3.09				
				75	7.46	5.12	6.96
40	3.21	3.17	3.13	76	7.66	5.13	7.23
41	3.25	3.22	3.17	77	7.86	5.14	7.50
42	3.30	3.26	3.22	78	8.05	5.15	7.81
43	3.36	3.31	3.26	79	8.23	5.15	8.12
44	3.41	3.36	3.31	†80	8.40	5.15	8.47
45	3.47	3.41	3.36	*and under		†and over	

Chapter 5

Other Forms of Savings and Insurance

ANOTHER KIND OF INSURANCE THAT IS PARTICULARLY POPULAR among the younger couples who are buying homes and planning for security in their old ages is mortgage insurance. It insures the life of the family breadwinner and is designed to pay off the mortgage in the event of his death. Unlike other insurance policies, the value of this one *decreases* as time goes on. That's because under the normal monthly amortization mortgage the longer a family head lives, the less he owes the bank on his mortgage.

These are usually written for ten, fifteen, twenty, twenty-five, and thirty years, and are called mortgage redemption policies. They're earmarked to pay off the *balance* of a mortgage in the event the borrower does not live to do so himself. In addition, it usually provides a cash balance for taxes or improvements.

At the end of the "mortgage period," when the note has been paid off, there's a fair amount of money left over which can be converted to a paid-up life insurance policy, taken in cash, used for extended insurance, or can be continued as permanent life insurance protection at a reduced annual premium.

Suppose you have a mortgage on your home for $10,000 and you're thirty-four years of age. You have agreed to pay this off in twenty years with regular monthly amortization payments. You take out a mortgage redemption policy worth, initially, $10,000. It's going to be worth about $500 *less* each year for twenty years, because you owe the bank about $500 less each year. But at the end of twenty years you have an accumulated value of $3800.

So, at the age of fifty-four, with no more mortgage on your home, you can elect to do the following:

—Take a paid-up policy worth $2124 with no further payments whatsoever, plus a bonus of $786.60 in cash, representing accumulated dividends.

—Extend the $3800 worth of life insurance protection for seventeen years and two hundred days without any further payments of premiums.

—Take $1384.15 of guaranteed cash value, plus the accumulated dividends, of course.

—Continue $3800 of permanent life insurance at a reduced annual premium.

Roughly speaking, such a policy would cost about $130 a year for the first twenty years, if written for a healthy man of thirty-four. After twenty years, if he elects to continue $3800 worth of permanent life insurance, it would cost him about $100 a year. Actually, if the dividends were permitted to accumulate with the company, the policy of $3800 would be fully paid up in about twenty-four years.

There are many other forms of insurance. You may want to shop around. Veterans, converting their GI insurance from term, may prefer something other than the whole-life or ordinary life coverage. Those buying insurance from companies may find another type of insurance more suited to their personal plans than whole life.

Some may want to look into annuities which provide monthly income for life after a certain age.

Some may prefer endowment policies which pay off after a

certain length of time (particularly useful for children who will one day require money for educational purposes).

Some may want "retirement insurance" which is a variation of the two mentioned above, tied in with Social Security benefits to provide retirement income.

Just remember that insurance is a lifetime program. It little behooves a policyholder to change his policies around after he has had them for a few years. Before you buy, learn all you can about the product you're buying. If you don't like your agent, get another. Write to your company, to the State Insurance Department or the local Life Underwriters Association. The central clearing agency for basic information about insurance is the Institute of Life Insurance, 275 Park Avenue, New York, New York 10017. This outfit is maintained as a public service. Its work in your behalf will be factual, prompt, courteous—and free of charge.

Before leaving the subject of insurance, it would be beneficial to consider one other kind of insurance: liability.

The more you save, the more you have, the greater is the risk of losing it. Liability insurance is one way of protecting what you have toiled so hard to accumulate.

The wealthier you become or the more important you become in your job and community, the more liable you are to be sued by someone. Under ordinary circumstances, someone falling on the ice in front of your home and suffering a leg fracture would be content to have you pay for the medical and hospital bills plus compensation for lost time at work. But not if it's believed that you have a substantial savings account, or that you own most of your home, or that you have an ambitious insurance program. Let such an idea gain any currency, and you'll be sued like a Morgan or Vanderbilt.

The same holds true if you have a job with glamour or prominence attached to it. A classic example would be a radio or TV announcer, someone whose voice is known to the entire community. Though he toils hard for comparatively low reward, just like anyone else, such a person is believed by the general public to be royally paid—and he would be sued accordingly in the event of any mishap.

Without further illustration it seems sufficient to point out that liability insurance in liberal amounts is worthwhile protection for the money that is accumulated with such pain and patience.

Another form of insurance you may want to investigate is savings-bank life insurance, offered in four states: New York, Pennsylvania, Massachusetts, and Connecticut. The banks offer it with "low overhead," no agents, no fees, no commission, no collection costs, thus frequently can sell up to $25000 worth of protection cheaper than the regular insurance companies can. Sometimes the nonforfeiture provisions for loans and cash surrenders are also more favorable. It is worth-while investigating if you live in one of those states. It's available in most savings banks.

No discussion of saving could be complete without a repetition of the great values to be found in savings bonds. They're the "safest" form of savings—safe because they're backed by the United States government. They can always be redeemed on demand, at the stated value.

Most people probably know it already, since they're so popular, but it's worth restating that savings bonds now bear a higher yield of interest and a better return in the early years of the bond.

Chapter 6

Ground Rules for Saving

THE PURPOSE OF THE PRECEDING CHAPTERS IS TO INSTILL IN THE reader an appreciation of the value of savings and to dispel some of the misconceptions about the perils to the saver in the "fluctuations" of the economic system.

We have discussed how—and where—to save:

1. Save *cash* regularly, in a bank, in a Savings and Loan Association, or in some other safe place.

2. Save with savings bonds.

3. Save through insurance.

4. Save with real estate.

The major difficulty, the average reader will find, comes in launching a real savings program.

The first step in that direction should be a thorough and critical look at the family budget. Cut it to essentials without scrimping. Then:

—Set up an inflexible savings program, so much each payday, to go into a bank or into savings bonds (or alternate between the two).

—Buy just as much life insurance as you can afford, of a type that will best suit your long-range plan.

These are the first tottering steps toward security. One learns to walk before competing for the four-minute mile. It is enough to try this program for size for a while, to get it comfortably broken in.

Then, when your savings program is functioning smoothly, efficiently, and to your own satisfaction, consider the next big step toward financial independence, the purchase of real estate.

You may want to use some of your accumulated savings for a down payment—*some* of your savings, not all. Leave enough to cushion yourself against unexpected demands for money.

Again, *reach* for your new home; buy just as much of a home as you can afford, for it's good business.

Once you've made this final obligation on your income, you'll be embarked on as sound and as well-rounded a savings program as a working man or woman can establish.

After that it's up to you. You must decide when to increase the amount of your regular savings, when to buy more insurance, when to buy more savings bonds.

With each increase in income, there should be a corresponding increase in the *ratio* of savings. If you're saving 10 per cent of your salary and you get a $10 raise, you should increase the amount of your savings by $1.00.

When you're tempted to cheat a little bit, to skimp on the savings, just remember that you're cheating no one but yourself and your own retirement plan.

There will come a point, not too long after you have got your full savings program running, when it may be wise to do a little investing, timidly at first, and with profound care.

In later chapters we will discuss the timing on this, and the extent to which you should enter the investment field.

First, however, it is necessary to study the stock market and to understand it. Even if you are already an investor, it behooves you to read the next few chapters with care, for no one really "knows" the market, and any review of its functions should be beneficial.

First, learn *how* to invest, then *why* to invest, then *when* to invest. This is the order decreed by the wisest minds in Wall Street to be the proper way to absorb the skills of the science of investment.

Part II

Invest It

Chapter 7

Making Money in the Market

THE STOCK MARKET IS NOT WHAT MANY PEOPLE THINK IT IS. INVESTING in stocks is not as risky as many people say it is.

It is not *easy* to make money in Wall Street. There's no magic formula. No dopesters have worked out any provable or proved "systems." Everyone who invests in stocks takes losses at one time or another. The trick is not how to win all the time—it's how to keep losses at a minimum and to win *most* of the time.

The trick is not to invest: anyone can *invest*. The way to success is through speculation or what, to the public, *seems* like speculation.

To do this the speculator must have an intimate knowledge of the stock market and the functions of the stock exchanges, a great deal of information about the corporation whose stock he is buying, and ability to make an appraisal of the economy and the commercial markets of the nation.

It sounds like an overwhelming job, and a task with many complications. The truth is, it's neither backbreaking nor unduly complicated.

It does not require "contacts" on Wall Street. It does not require membership in the Brokers' Club, Lawyers' Club, Wall Street Club, or friends at the Sleepy Hollow Country Club.

It requires a pair of workable eyes to read with and a brain trained sufficiently to exercise good judgment.

The speculator in Evanston, Illinois, or Clearwater, Florida, is more likely to do a good job of investing his money than the so-called insider on Wall Street, because the out-of-towners are not exposed to the tipsters or dopesters, nor to the sheep-herd movements of the Wall Street flock.

It is not possible to move with the pack and speculate successfully. Yet the movements of the majority must be considered, and the safe speculator has to move with the majority for certain lengths of time.

It was Bernard Baruch, I think, who said, "Buy 'em when they're low and sell 'em when they're high."

Stocks are not *low* unless a majority of traders does not want them. They're not *high* unless a majority desires them.

So for some purposes the successful speculator must move contrarily when he buys, and then go along with the majority opinion up to the point where he sells.

It is necessary to have a basic knowledge of the workings of that city of banks, brokers, and stone towers known as Wall Street, the name of one of the smaller and less pretentious alleys in the bustling financial district at the tip of Manhattan. There are two stock exchanges there, the mighty New York Stock Exchange and the active American Stock Exchange, formerly called the Curb Exchange.

Neither the New York Stock Exchange nor the American Stock Exchange owns any stock or sells any stock. The function of the exchanges is merely to provide physical facilities for the auctioning off of securities, and for the rapid recording of prices and the speedy transmission of those prices to other parts of the country and the world. The exchanges set the trading rules, establish the hours of trading, and police the ethics and conduct of the brokers who constitute the exchange membership.

It is with the brokers that the investor deals. These are the people who act as "middle men" in the sale of stock. They may own the stock they sell to you, but usually they buy it for you on the trading floor or the exchange where the stock is "listed." They buy it at auction, bidding the price you have instructed them to offer for it.

It is the brokers who maintain the "board-rooms" where stock prices are displayed throughout the trading hours. They also have "back rooms" which few outsiders see, where there are complicated but efficient procedures for speeding the records of stock transactions and for effecting the transfer of stocks that have been bought or sold for the broker's customers.

Brokers charge a commission when a stock is sold. It is a small commission which fluctuates with two factors: the price and the number of shares involved.

Without this setup of stock exchanges and brokers many of America's largest corporations would not have been able to be so large—and in fact many of them would not have been able to exist.

Roughly speaking, here's what happened when XYZ Corporation, manufacturer of electronic devices, decided to expand its operation, how it affected Wall Street, and what it meant to you, both as an investor and as a consumer:

It was a couple of years ago that the sales manager told the board of directors of XYZ Corporation that if they could improve their line of electronic devices to include a printed circuitry for television sets, he was sure they could capture the vast market that seemed to be opening in that field. The board was impressed and soon charged the research director with the responsibility of developing the circuits and devising a way to mass-produce it at a reasonable price.

About a year and a half later the research director announced himself satisfied with the results. He had produced a number of circuits. They had been tested and found satisfactory. His department had worked out a method of mass production. The sales manager had sampled the market and found it strong. The production engineer had completed his report—everything was ready.

The various reports were presented to the board of directors.

Only one thing gave them pause. The production engineer's report called for a new building, many new and expensive machines, the hiring of several hundred skilled employees, and, because of the newness of the product, the creation of a supplementary selling operation.

He appraised the total cost at something like $8,000,000.

That was all right by the directors, since the sales manager's report showed that the $8,000,000 could be recovered in a relatively short time and that the market for the circuits would go on for quite a while. Further, the research director indicated that there were numerous other things that could be made profitably on the equipment the production manager wanted to order.

It seemed like a good investment. But the corporation didn't have $8,000,000 lying idle. All of its money was tied up in production equipment and inventory. Fortunately there was some authorized but unissued common stock—saved by the directors for just such an occasion. Also, they could *borrow* some of the money.

That's how they came to apply to the Securities and Exchange Commission for permission to issue 88,000 shares of stock at $50 a share and to sell $4,000,000 worth of bonds.

The directors wanted to raise $4,000,000 through the sale of the stock. The brokers would want a commission of $5.00 a share, which would cost an additional $400,000, so instead of issuing 80,000 shares which would raise the $4,000,000, they asked permission to issue 88,000 shares to raise $4,400,000.

They filed a registration statement with the Securities and Exchange Commission and prepared for submission to the SEC a detailed report of just why they wanted the money and what they intended to do with it, together with a report on the present financial structure of the company. This latter document is called a prospectus.

The SEC assigned a staff to investigate the accuracy of all the statements. After receiving a favorable report, the commission gave approval to go ahead with the sale of the stock.

A group of brokers got together and bought all the stock at $45 a share. Then they arranged for a "New Offering," that is, they put the stock "on the market" for the first time. Its offering price was $50. Since the stock already issued by the corporation was selling on the free market for $53 a share, this seemed like a very good buy to the investors of the nation and all 88,000 shares of the stock were sold in a few hours' time.

That accounted for $4,000,000.

The remaining $4,000,000 was to be raised through the issuing of bonds. The XYZ Corporation initially went through the same steps of clearance with the SEC. The bond offering was approved and it became a very attractive issue. The company agreed to pay 5½ per cent annually and to redeem the bonds in ten years' time. They then became known as XYZ's 83's (because they were to be paid back in 1983).

This illustrates, perhaps too simply, the difference between a stock and a bond. A stock is a share of the ownership of a corporation. A bond is a promissory note, evidence of indebtedness. The person who bought a share of stock in XYZ Corporation became one of the owners of the company. The person who bought a bond became one of the creditors of the company—he loaned his money to XYZ Corporation in exchange for their promise to pay him back, at specific rates of interest, over a specific period of time.

The bonds were sold in much the same way that the stocks were sold. They were bought by underwriters who then merchandised them to investors at a slight markup in price. They were priced at 100—or $100 per bond—and were sold in lots of ten bonds per lot. In other words it required at least $1000 to get in on the bonds, while it took only $50 to get a share of stock.

Regard, then, the results to the economy and the people as the result of XYZ's sortie into Wall Street.

The corporation expanded. It bought several million dollars' worth of machinery, placing huge orders in the machine tool building plants in Springfield, Vermont, Providence, Rhode Island, and Cleveland and Cincinnati, Ohio. It ordered vast quantities of raw materials for its circuits, condensers from Brooklyn, wire from Philadelphia, rubber coating material from Akron, steel from Pittsburgh, tungsten from Denver, glass from Chicago, cardboard boxes for shipping from Portland, Maine.

Indirectly, the XYZ expansion gave work to thousands, perhaps hundreds of thousands of American workers.

Directly, XYZ Corporation hired several hundred more industrial workers to produce the circuits.

Around the country the savers who had accumulated some money and were looking for a good investment bought up the stocks and subscribed to the bonds. This gave employment to the thousands directly involved in the brokerage houses and on the stock exchanges.

In the television industry, where competition is tough, a dozen set manufacturers revised their programs to take into account the advent of the new circuits produced by XYZ Corporation. They, too, hired additional help. They put on large selling and advertising campaigns.

Their money went into "distribution." It went to newspapers and magazines, radio and television, to advertising agencies and public relations organizations, to warehouses and railroads and trucking companies. In addition, of course, they, too, bought heavily from their suppliers of raw materials so that they could produce the new type TV sets.

And all over the country, regardless of whether they were directly affected or not, Americans benefited in two ways: *1.* As consumers they had available to them a better television set, giving better performance; and *2.* As residents of the nation they shared in the general prosperity created initially by the issuance of stock and bonds which, like good will, multiplied and spread across the face of the land. For when the distributors and retailers got the new sets, they, too, prospered, and so did their clerks and workers, and so did the banks and the grocers, and so on, *ad infinitum.*

All this, because of Wall Street. All this because of the existence of the stock exchanges and this nation's "investment system."

It is exciting to participate in it.

Since the end of World War II the participation by Americans has been increasing. No one knows just how many persons own stock, but a survey by the Brookings Institution, made at the behest of the New York Stock Exchange, put the ownership at something more than 6,500,000 in 1955. It is believed to be 35,-000,000 in 1972. It's fairly widely distributed, with the residents of both seaboards being more active participants. Ownership is divided nearly evenly between the sexes. Men own 50.2 per cent and women 49.8 per cent of the securities.

Were it not for the two huge exchanges, both located in New York's financial district, it is doubtful that there would be such wide ownership of the securities of the nation's top corporations.

There are other stock exchanges which function more or less on a regional basis—Boston Stock Exchange, Midwest Exchange (Chicago), San Francisco Stock Exchange, Baltimore–Philadelphia Stock Exchange, etc. However, it is the two largest exchanges in New York where qualified securities are first registered and where, as a result, most of the trading is done. Mechanically, both exchanges operate the same way. Neither is a profit-making organization. Both are maintained primarily to provide the physical facilities for a speedy and accurate auction market, an auction market for the ownership shares of the nation's corporations.

At the corner of Broad and Wall streets is the giant New York Stock Exchange, as bustling as Grand Central Terminal and as accessible to the public. It is a huge granite building dedicated to the basic law—the law of supply and demand. And the demands of the farmer with a few hundred dollars in Davenport,

Iowa, or the traveling businessman in Paris, France, are met just as rapidly and with the same efficiency as the demands of the millionaire investor whose office abuts the Stock Exchange on Wall Street. The Iowa farmer has merely to call the branch office of a brokerage firm to place his order for a few shares of, say, du Pont stock, and within a matter of minutes the purchase has been made on the "trading floor" of the Exchange and Farmer Jones is no longer just a farmer, he's one of the owners of E. I. du Pont de Nemours and Company of Wilmington, Delaware! He's a manufacturer of chemicals, textiles, paints, explosives, cellophane, synthetic fibers, and a hundred other products.

The farmer who wanted du Pont stock didn't have to look for someone with du Pont stock to sell. He didn't have to advertise for it or make the rounds of a series of brokerage offices. He didn't have to write to Wilmington, Delaware, to find out how much the stock was worth.

He needed only to call his broker to get a "quote" on the du Pont stock. He knew, immediately, whether the price was right and fair. Once his decision was made to buy, the transaction was sped on its way and, as the efficient machinery of the Stock Exchange went into operation, he was made one of the owners of du Pont Corporation.

It would have taken much more effort to buy part interest in a variety store in his own home town!

Here's how it worked:

The Davenport farmer, Mr. Jones, had sold a crop at a good profit and after paying his debts and putting aside enough cash to last until the next "cash crop" came along, he found he had some money left over, money he wanted to invest.

He went to a broker's office right there in Davenport. The office is a branch of the Wall Street firm whose members "own seats" on the exchange. This is an expression handed down from the old days when exchange members actually had to sit while the president read off the list of securities offered for sale.

The Davenport representative of the commission house

talked it over with Mr. Jones and determined that the basic desire of Mr. Jones was not to make an immediate "killing" in Wall Street, but to invest his money over the long-range period in a stock that was relatively "safe," paying regular dividends at a good rate, and deemed to be a good investment.

They discussed several stocks until finally the broker mentioned du Pont. "It's certainly a good stock," he told Mr. Jones. "As you know, the company is highly successful and has a long history of successes. It pays a good dividend, regularly, and moreover, it's a chemical company, and the chemical industry still has an interesting growth potential. In addition, du Pont owns a number of shares, though by no means a controlling interest, in General Motors and U. S. Rubber—so actually, by owning du Pont stock you can benefit from three or more corporations."

This appealed to Mr. Jones, so the representative filled out a query slip, handed it to a girl teletypist, and a wire was sped to the New York office asking for a "quote" on du Pont.

In New York the broker's main office telephoned the exchange's quotation department where current up-to-the-split-second quotations on all listed securities are received by direct wires from each trading post on the floor of the exchange.

Each stock is assigned a particular location at one of the eighteen posts on the trading floor. All transactions in a stock must take place at its assigned post.

Here, at a post, each bid and each offer must be quoted *aloud.* With about 1500 stocks listed on the New York Stock Exchange, it can be imagined that there is a confusing din around each post—but it's smoothly ordered confusion, and each yelp of a trader means something to his fellow traders.

The quote on the price of a stock comes from these shouted offers and bids and is recorded instantly in the quotation department of the exchange. It was from here that Farmer Jones' quotation on du Pont stock originated, and which reached him seconds later in Davenport, Iowa.

Farmer Jones was not a rich man. He could not afford 100

shares of du Pont stock. Normally, shares are sold in "block" of 100. So his broker's agent, acting for Farmer Jones, bought him 40 shares of du Pont from an odd-lot dealer. For this there is a charge of one eighth of a point or (12½ cents) per share, going to the odd lot dealer. But under exchange rules the odd-lot dealer cannot refuse to sell the du Pont stock if he has it—nor can he refuse to buy it back in the event Farmer Jones ever wants to sell it.

This small charge of one eighth of a point is typical of the small commissions charged by Stock Exchange members. Commissions are the lowest for the transfer of any property.

Chapter 8

Becoming a Wise Investor

BECAUSE ANYWHERE FROM 30,000,000 TO 35,000,000 AMERICANS own stock at any given time, there exists in Wall Street and other financial centers across the land, a substantial and rather well-paid army of generic soothsayers known as "analysts." As in any army there are many ranks and many degrees of importance and responsibility.

It is the design of these technicians to supply information and advice on:

1. The condition of the nation's economy.
2. The health or lack of it in any corporation.
3. The expectations for any particular industry.
4. The trend of the stock market and the relationship of the foregoing to stock prices.

Because Wall Street, partly for convenience and partly through a profound emphasis on traditionalism, has developed and maintained numerous terms indigenous to the district, these analysts seem to converse in a language all their own, like medical doctors or scientists. In many cases their advices are imparted in the lingo of their own cult, to the confusion and dismay of those who have freshly sought their services.

It's an easy language to master, however, and with a little patience and practice almost anyone can pick it up and in a short time will be conversing in "Wallstreetese" along with the natives.

I would not disparage the analytical and advisory services of the reputable brokerage houses of Wall Street, and the writings of their experts are available to the public, usually free, through the branch offices in any city.

Where do the experts get their "dope"? There are no crystal balls in the financial district, nor are there many "insiders" with information of unusual significance.

In the broad scope the analysts get their information from the same sources open to anyone—the newspapers and technical periodicals. They read with interest all of the economic, business, financial, and industrial news, and then they relate it to their own thinking, to their own interpretations.

In specifics, when they deal with particular corporations or individual securities, they are relating facts which they or their technicians learned by talking with the officials of the company.

There is no reason why any investor cannot be his own analyst when it comes to the broad considerations of the economy and the market. All he needs to do is "study" his newspapers and trade journals. Then he can be as well informed as any one else.

But in considering the specifics, it's good to have the assistance of the Wall Street analysts, for they have facilities (and the time) for getting at the pertinent facts about a special corporation or a particular industry.

By reading the newspapers anyone can have a fairly good idea of whether the upcoming three months or six months are to be more prosperous or less prosperous.

By reading the newspapers and applying a little common sense, anyone can have a fairly good idea which industries are going to be the busiest in the months ahead and therefore which companies stand to make the most profit.

Then the trick is to get the advice of a broker or professional analyst on the particular company best suited to you for an investment.

Certainly it took no genius, once the atomic bomb had been exploded and it had been revealed that uranium was the source of its energy, to know that the companies equipped to explore for and reclaim uranium ore were in line for some profitable expansion. It took keen professional analytical ability, however, to know which of the numerous companies so equipped were most likely to succeed.

Thus, whether you're buying for investment or speculation, the fundamental procedure is the same. First you determine which industry you want to put your money into, and then which company in that industry. You will do well to get help, professional help, in making the second selection.

At this point we can accept a couple of premises. The first is basic: If the capitalistic system is to function, then we must have a stock market to raise the capital needed to run our corporations, large and small. The second is this: If the capitalistic system is good, so is the system of marketing stocks. A third we might consider is this: If the stock market continues successfully to function jointly as a source of capital for industry and as a refuge for the savings of our people, then it must be a pretty good place for you to put some of your savings. If it were not a good place for savings, it would not have functioned so successfully for so many years.

It would be simple for this writer or for any other to interview a number of Wall Street professional analysts and to set down a number of rules so that you could try to be your own analyst. However, I believe that not all of us can be good analysts any more than all of us can be good nuclear physicists, or all women be good mothers.

What we can be is good investors.

To be a good investor you must acquire a certain frame of mind, starting, perhaps, with the *will* to save, which in time grows into the *will* to invest. It means reading the newspapers and news magazines with a new attitude, with more than the mere desire to be informed. You must have a desire to interpret what you learn in terms of the effect it will have on business and industry in general, and on certain businesses and industries in particular. How will the new tariff bill (I'll wager there will be a new bill before Congress whenever you read this book) affect the textile industry or the hardware industry or the food processing industry?

Once a person acquires the proper frame of mind, he's an investor, and being an investor means, perforce, that he's enough of an analyst to do all that he needs to do before consulting a professional.

The prospective investor should be like an *adult* in a toy store. A child in the toy store would find that his money was burning a hole in his pocket and he might buy anything. An adult, however, would probably shop selectively and come out with a good purchase. So it should be with stock buying.

You have saved regularly, and you are still doing so. You have a good insurance program, you have a good home. Now you move on to the next step in the program that rewards you with independence. Now you invest in stocks. How? When? How much? These are important things for you to know.

Chapter 9

Now You Invest It

IT IS NOT NECESSARY TO *SAVE* YOUR WAY TO INDEPENDENCE, OR SAVE enough to purchase your security, before you become an investor in the stock market. We are basing our plan here on the premise that you *buy* your independence and security, but the ideal program is one in which the medium of the securities market plays an early role.

In short, one need not be a millionaire to become an investor who reaps good returns from the stock market. For the purposes of security, independence, and eventual retirement, a millionaire doesn't need the good yields of the stock market. He already possesses independence.

If your savings program is well organized, if your insurance program is in good shape, if you own a home or are well programmed in that respect, then you can—and should—become an investor in the stock market.

After a person has acquired adequate insurance and a cash reserve fund, there is no better way to build up a retirement fund than regular periodic buying of good common stocks. The only trick is to know which are the good ones.

The emphasis should first be on "good" common stocks, not necessarily the "blue chips" or securities of high "investment" quality, but rather stocks of good companies in so-called "growth" industries—industries which have a past record and possess prospects which indicate future expansion at a faster rate than the average.

So when do you start? As soon as you can spare the money, for investing embodies some risks.

Buying stock is not gambling. It's not hazarding your resources as in horse racing or other types of betting. In a horse race, for instance, you pick one of a group of horses and bet that he will come in first, second, or third. If you guess wrong, you lose your money.

In the stock market you do not have so many odds against you.

If you pick a good stock selling at 20 (that is, $20 a share) which is yielding a 25-cent quarterly dividend (or $1.00 a year, which is 5 per cent of your investment) you are protected in two ways:

First, even if the price of the stock falls, say, to $18, you do not care because if the dividend remains the same, you will still be getting 5 per cent on your investment.

Second, if the stock goes higher and you sell at, say, $25, after a year, you have really gained $6.00 per share because you'll be getting $5.00 per share more than you paid for it, plus the $1.00 per share you earned in dividends during the year.

The point is, you can guess wrong about a stock and have it decrease in value, but it is really no loss to you unless you sell. Furthermore, it is rare, indeed, when a legitimate stock worth $20 becomes absolutely worthless and you lose your entire investment as you do in a horse race.

There is just no comparison, and those who say investing is gambling are voicing their ignorance.

Nevertheless, there is risk in investing. Your money is not "safe" or "guaranteed" as it is in a bank where your deposits are insured against loss. But that's why your rewards are much higher than they are in a bank where your gain is limited to the rate of interest paid by the bank.

Anyone who does not believe the stock market will go higher over the years does not really believe in the future growth of America, for the growth of stock prices and the growth of America's economy are synonymous, and nearly simultaneous. If we retain the capitalistic system, as we have refined it, no one can be bearish about America's economic future.

Many of the professionals of Wall Street, when called upon to advise newcomers to the investment market, say that if you haven't much money to "play with," then it is proper to buy stocks for long-range gains. These they call "investment" stocks, as opposed to "speculative" stocks.

In essence this is sound advice, although it's a form of semantics that isn't really too helpful. For all stocks are "speculative" stocks. There's no such thing as a guaranteed "investment" as opposed to speculation. Anyone who buys a share of stock is speculating—speculating on its future value.

There are shadings of qualities, however, and it is these delicate tones that soon intrigue the investor.

For instance, American Telephone & Telegraph Company stock might well be considered an "investment" because it is a matter of record that for two generations this giant of the utilities paid a constant dividend of $9.00 annually. Anyone buying AT&T can be reasonably confident that he'll get a dividend on his investment.

But AT&T is a blue chip, as are many of the other topflight corporations with glamorous dividend and earnings records, such as du Pont, General Electric, General Motors, Standard Oil of New Jersey, etc. Over the long haul any of these are likely to prove "good investments."

Perhaps the difference between "investment" and "speculation" could be summed up this way: An investment is a stock purchased for its dividends and long-term gain, thus a stock which will be held for a long period; a speculative stock is one which is purchased because the buyer believes its price will rise in the near future, and thus it is a stock which will be held but a short time.

So what does the new investor buy—investment stocks or speculative stocks?

It depends, of course, on how much money he has available at the time. The average person of average income who is interested in a program of saving it, and investing it so he might buy independence and hence retirement, wants two things from the stock market.

When he first starts to invest, he's much more interested in the long-term gain than he is in immediate profits, for he's looking some years ahead toward his retirement. Yet, somewhere along the line, he must substantially increase his working capital by turning some good profits in the stock market, for he knows that the earnings from his job will hardly provide him with a backlog of security in his old age.

It seems sensible to me to start inauspiciously by buying the good, seasoned common stocks and that includes some blue chips. In this way you can operate in the market as you become more familiar with it. One need not be an expert to buy some of the veteran stocks, for any broker knows all about them and can tell you their prospects with fair accuracy. You'll be anything but a "plunger," but your money will be relatively safe and you'll be getting yourself off to a fine start.

The second emphasis should be on diversification to whatever extent is practicable considering the amount of money available for investment. It is not smart to put all your eggs in one basket, particularly if you're buying for the long haul. You want to be spread over as many industries as possible, for some industries will get spurts of growth and large profits while others lag somewhat.

It is true that no substantial segment of the nation's complex economy can be depressed while others prosper, yet common

sense tells you that over a five-or ten-year period some industries will leap ahead while others either mark time or walk
slowly. For instance, we know that big things lie ahead in the
field of atomic energy. Yet big things lie ahead in the world of
chemistry too. And what can we expect from the automobile
industry or the relatively small but important automobile parts
and equipment manufacturers?

Diversification for the small investor, the wage or salary
earner, could be achieved by investing the first accumulation
of savings in one stock, the next accumulation of savings in a
different stock, and preferably in a different industry, and each
successive accumulation of savings in still another industry.
This need not be a hard-and-fast rule which cannot be broken.
If something looks especially good to you at the time you have
an accumulation of savings ready for investment, it need not be
turned down just because you already own securities in a company in that industry. But for the broad range it's good policy.

As with the habit of savings, I would emphasize regularity
when it comes to investing. Common stocks of good companies
are generally good investments, but a program of regular, periodic investment will ordinarily show far better results than
hit-or-miss investing whenever "extra" funds are available.

The reason for this is that as stock prices fluctuate, and even
the best of them rise and fall in price, the investor will be
buying stocks when the prices are high and when prices are
low, but because he is investing a fixed number of dollars with
regularity, he will be buying a larger number of shares when
prices are low than when they are high.

Here, then, is the trick. You invest a certain number of *dollars*
at regular intervals, and you get as many shares as the money
will buy. You are not so concerned with the *number of shares*
as with the number of dollars, for the number of shares will
change from time to time.

The next recommendation is basic: Let your dividends buy
more stock for you. Don't spend them as the checks come in.

Since you are building a nest egg, a fund to produce income in later years, your concern is more with the future than the present. Plowing back present income from your stocks will speed the growth of the fund. In fact, after ten or twelve years the dividends reinvested each year might well be a larger total than the savings invested each year. And that will be the day you have won!

The day you reinvest *more* in dividends than you have been able to save, you are putting your feet on the last roadway to success. From that point on the job is easier and the goal is in sight.

In 1956, this writer asked Winthrop H. Smith, then the managing partner of the giant brokerage house of Merrill Lynch, Pierce, Fenner & Beane (now it's Merrill Lynch, Pierce, Fenner & Smith) how a person would fare if he saved only $25 a month, or $300 a year and invested that $300 a year, plus his accumulated dividends, on the first marketing day of each New York.

Mr. Smith, of course, couldn't project into the future. He had to consider the past, for which there were definite records. He went back thirteen years to 1944 and took the hypothetical $300 and "invested" it in the stocks comprising the Dow-Jones industrial average. This, in fact, is impossible to do, since the Dow-Jones Industrials comprise 30 selected industrial stocks whose value is computed daily to permit comparison of a representative group of industrial stocks by the investing community. Nevertheless, since they *are* representative stocks, the $300 investment in Dow Jones Industrials gives a very good illustration of how it can work.

Even though this table was completed nearly twenty years ago, it remains valid today. The one difference should be that the investor could today save more than $25 per month.

Here is Mr. Smith's table:

Result of 13-Year Purchase Program
Based on Dow Jones Industrial Averages
with Dividends Reinvested

	Savings to Invest Jan. 1	Dividends Received Previous Year	Total to Invest Jan. 1	Market Value of Stk. Owned Jan. 2 Each Year*	Dow Jones Industrials Jan. 2
1944	$300	. . .	$300	$295	136.09
1945	300	$14	314	639	152.21
1946	300	28	328	1132	192.50
1947	300	44	344	1381	177.29
1948	300	72	372	1775	180.94
1949	300	155	413	2139	176.65
1950	300	155	455	2871	199.93
1951	300	232	532	3913	235.89
1952	300	271	571	5038	269.58
1953	300	289	589	6047	292.41
1954	300	333	633	6434	280.96
1955	300	400	700	9983	405.83
1956	300	531	831	12,858	489.45

*Deduction made for brokerage commissions.

Dividends received during the year—*any* year—were assumed to have been added to the $300 invested at the beginning of the next year. Allowance was made for brokerage commissions.

On a total ten-year investment of $3000, the program finishes the period with stocks worth $6047!

If you were told, today, that by saving $25 a month for ten years you could be virtually assured of having *at least* $6047 at the end of the ten-year period, would you be willing to do it?

Can you think of an easier way, involving less risk, to double your money in such a short time?

You can see from the tabulation that by the end of the ten-year period the annual dividends have just about equaled the $300 annual contribution from savings. Certainly $289 is not enough to retire on, but the assumption is that most people would expect to save up for retirement over a much longer period than ten years.

An investment of $300 a year for twenty-five years would total $7500.

If you apply the same mathematics to the twenty-five-year period as demonstrated in the chart for a ten-year period, you come up with some very lively figures.

For example, with the market appreciation (the increase in the value of stocks) and the reinvestment of dividends sustained at the same average rate shown in the ten-year tabulation, your $25-a-month investment over a twenty-five year period would grow to a fund which would produce an annual income *from dividends alone* of $1500 to $2000.

Naturally this wouldn't provide retirement, but imagine how it would work when applied as a supplement to other retirement income (which will be discussed in later chapters) and to Federal Old Age benefits or annuities!

Obviously it is not possible to invest in the Dow Jones or any other averages (there are three other important ones: Standard & Poor's, and New York *Times* averages), but the table does suggest what the probable result would have been if a small investor had followed a program of buying stocks from 1944 through 1954.

A table could have been compiled on the basis of purchases of individual stocks, and no doubt it would have been interesting to many newcomers to the stock market to see which ones had been selected by the "experts." However, such a computation would have been open to criticism that the individual stocks have been hand-picked by hindsight to prove the point that it's profitable to invest in the market.

Winthrop Smith said that if careful selection had been made (on the basis of advice from qualified sources) of stocks of the type he believed should be used in a program of this kind, he felt strongly that even better results could have been shown.

To recapitulate, here are the main considerations before you invest in an investment program:

1. Buy good common stocks.

2. Diversify your holdings—buy as widely separated stocks as, for instance, a chemical company, a farm machinery company, and an oil company.

3. Buy your stocks regularly, at regularly stated intervals.

4. Reinvest the dividends that you earn from your stocks.

5. Accumulate your savings over a regular period to permit regular periodic investment.

I would like to emphasize here that unless you want to do it the long, hard way, you cannot expect to merely *save* enough to provide for your retirement.

Compare this with the possibilities embodied in the preceding table of investments.

If you merely *saved* your money you would, in ten years, have $3000 (saving $25 a month), plus interest.

If you invested it in the theoretical Dow Jones Industrials, you'd have $6047 in the same period.

The point being made here is that while a good and constant savings program is necessary, it is, alone, not enough. If you stick with savings only, you will be operating with an underutilized program. Savings is Step #1. Investing in higher-yielding things such as real estate and the stock market, is Step #2.

Responding slowly, interest rates on savings accounts do reflect inflation. When you own stocks, you will see that *on average* both stock prices and dividends respond much more quickly to inflationary pressures and *increase* more rapidly as the purchasing power of the dollar *declines.*

Both savings and investments are needed to give yourself a program that is "defensible," both against recession (when your savings will be protected) and against inflation (when your stock market purchases, if wisely chosen, will keep pace with other rising prices).

Chapter 10

The Monthly Investment Plan

THERE ARE TWO CONVENIENT WAYS FOR THE PERSON OF SMALL AND moderate means to invest in common stocks without having to wait to accumulate an adequate sum. It is not necessary to save $25 a month until the end of the year when you can invest $300.

The New York Stock Exchange has arranged a plan with its member firms which permits anyone to buy stocks on a "Monthly Investment Plan," for a small amount of money each month.

Another way is to purchase shares in a mutual fund on a regular monthly plan which permits highly trained professionals to invest your money for you.

In this chapter we will deal with the first of these methods, the Monthly Investment Plan.

The Monthly Investment Plan is a belated application of America's wondrous invention of consumer credit to the stock market. The MIP will permit you to become a capitalist for as little as $10 down and $10 a week. With it you can share in the profits and buy into the ownership of America's corporations with small cash payments, just as, for years, you've been able to buy appliances and automobiles on the painless easy payment plan. You can buy stocks on a pay-as-you-go plan.

The planned purchase of stocks is no more difficult than the planned purchase of a washing machine.

Not all of the nearly 1400 brokers who are members of the New York Stock Exchange are equipped to handle the MIP, but a large majority of them can. It is probably the easiest way to acquire direct ownership of securities, and it may fit your own program better than the system of accumulating regular savings until you're ready to purchase stocks.

It's interesting to note that the MIP, an invention of the capitalists of Wall Street, was triggered by an idea from organized labor. G. Keith Funston, one time president of the New York Stock Exchange, had made a statement one day on the differences between Communists and Americans. "There is," he said, "no stock exchange in Moscow," a dynamic point to make in summing up the frustrations of the Russian workers, for they can never own a chunk of the businesses for which they labor.

A labor newspaper, *The Labor Union,* owned by the Dayton, Ohio, affiliates of the American Federation of Labor, praised Mr. Funston on making the point and ran a full-page editorial stating: ". . . we would like to sell you on the idea that your right and privilege to become an owner of American business, if you so choose, is one of those precious rights you enjoy and take for granted. And it's a right that you certainly wouldn't have if this country were controlled by Communists."

From this endorsement by labor, Funston was stimulated to create a plan which would make it easier for the average fellow of average income to own some of those shares of American business. Of this was born the Monthly Investment Plan.

It really isn't installment buying. An installment buyer gets his TV set, washing machine, or automobile delivered as soon as he contracts for it, and then pays for it while he's using it. Not so with pay-as-you-go stock purchases. You get them as you pay for them.

Let's say an accountant with an income of $15,000 a year decides he can put $50 a month aside for the purchase of stocks. He picks out a stock (XYZ Corporation) selling for $75 a share and decides he'd like to buy $1000 worth of this stock. So he goes to his broker and becomes a participant in the MIP.

After the accountant sends off his first month's payment of $50, the broker (or bank) credits his account with a $50 interest in one $75 share; thus he owns two thirds of a share of XYZ Corporation common stock. After payment of the second month's $50, the accountant would own outright one share of XYZ Corporation stock and have an interest or equity of $25 in a second share. Or to put it another way, he'd own one and one-third shares.

The first fully owned share would be sent to the accountant so that his name would appear on the corporation's records and he'd receive XYZ Corporation's annual reports and other company information, would be entitled to vote in company affairs as an owner, and, not to be overlooked, would receive any dividends.

If the corporation declared a dividend after the accountant made his first monthly payment but before he owned a full share of stock, his account would be credited with the equivalency of his ownership. In other words, since he owned two thirds of a share of stock after the first month of his MIP, he'd get two thirds of a dividend if one were paid that month. If it were a 75-cent dividend he'd get 50 cents credited to his account. (Of course, a stock costing $75 should yield more than a 75-cent quarterly dividend, for many good, secure stocks pay 8 per cent *per annum.*)

The accountant would not be committed to hold onto his stock. He could sell it whenever he wanted to. If the value of the stock should increase to, say, $85 a share he might want to sell his share, take his $10 profit, pay off the brokerage fees or service charges and come out with a net gain which could be reinvested at no cost. Or he could hold onto it as a good investment.

There's always the possibility that a stock will decline in value, but he can console himself that: *1.* His dividends are going to be the same, no matter the price of the stock; and *2.* His $50 payment next month will buy him a larger portion of a share.

It is as easy to open a Monthly Investment Plan account as it is to open a bank account. One needs only to visit a broker who handles MIP.

One of the great market places for investments is in over-the-counter securities, that is, stocks which are not listed or traded on either the New York Stock Exchange or the American Stock Exchange. Generally, the public has only skimpy knowledge of this huge market and is apt to believe that stocks traded over-the-counter (that is, not in public auction) are, somehow, really traded "under-the-counter" with some measure of slyness.

Nothing could be further from the truth. One of the first and most important facts about the over-the-counter market is that it is the world's largest market. There are 30,000 securities traded actively each day in the o-t-c market and the number of stocks listed on the New York Stock Exchange pales in comparison—a ratio in favor of the o-t-c market of about six to one.

Some of the outstanding corporations are represented in over-the-counter securities. *Time* magazine and *Life* magazine, for instance, are represented with the listing of Time, Inc., Diners Club, Pabst, American Express, and many others of equal corporate stature are traded over-the-counter, as are the stocks of almost every leading insurance company of the republic. So are the shares of mutual funds, whose functions and values are explained in detail in the next chapter.

There is a public misconception about the "liquidity" of the over-the-counter market which anyone investigating it will soon discover. Many believe that it is sometimes difficult to liquidate securities in the over-the-counter market, at least more difficult than it is to liquidate in the auction markets.

This is just not true.

Many general newspapers do not carry very extensive lists of quotations of over-the-counter stocks (the *New York Times* carries one of the largest lists) and this, perhaps, contributes to some reluctance on the part of the public to participate in over-the-counter purchases.

Actually, the National Association of Securities Dealers each day publishes what it calls its "pink sheets" giving latest quotes on bid and asked prices of over-the-counter stocks. Usually the brokers who handle orders for stock purchases on either of the two big exchanges also will handle purchases of over-the-counter securities. Such purchases are policed by tough regulations, including those of the Securities and Exchange Commission and the Department of Banking of each state.

Sometimes there is criticism of the wide "spread" between the bid prices and the asked prices listed in the newspapers or on the pink sheets for over-the-counter stocks. In most cases, it is my belief, this reflects the genuine earnestness of the o-t-c broker to quote the lowest bid available and the highest offering price available. A good broker dealing in over-the-counter securities feels obligated to "make a market" on new issues being offered to the public. I have seen it being done innumerable times. In other words, the broker does not sell his o-t-c securities to the public and then let prices find their own level. Usually, if the price is tending to sag, he will rush into the market and support it until the stock can stand on its own feet.

For this and numerous other reasons, the over-the-counter market is frequently spared the rather violent reactions in prices found in the securities listed on the major exchanges.

Chapter 11

Investing in a Mutual Fund

WE HAVE SHOWN THAT THE AVERAGE PERSON, IF HE IS TO PROVIDE for his own retirement, must pay *himself* out of his earnings during his productive years. The mere fact of putting money away regularly is important. But even more important is investing it sensibly and letting dividends accumulate so that your money works as hard for you as you have worked for it.

We have shown in preceding chapters that regular investing goes a long way toward reducing investment risks, for the investor gets an "average cost" over the years—his dollars buy more when stocks are lower; they buy higher value when stocks are higher.

We have also seen the advantages of diversified investing. Such advantages might be lost if investments are made in only a few securities, for they might be the "wrong" securities. By owning a diversified list of investments, the investor's fortunes depend upon a broad section of the leading companies of American industry.

Managed investing goes hand-in-hand with diversified investing. You can hire someone to do your investing for you.

Moreover, you can buy your way into a professionally managed fund. You can buy a portion of that fund and reap its benefits through dividends and appreciation in stock values proportionate to your interest and the size of your ownership of the fund. This is a mutual fund.

The advent of the mutual fund was based on the premise that the average fellow simply does not have the time, the knowledge, the ability, or the temperament to manage his own investments, particularly if he is to own a large and diversified list of securities. Thus, the mutual fund offers full-time professional investment management to pick your investments, watch them, and change them when necessary.

There are two types of mutual funds: open end funds and closed end funds. Technically speaking, the open end fund is a pure mutual fund and the closed end fund is an investment trust. Nevertheless, they are rarely so designated in ordinary conversation and in popular usage.

An open end fund, the standard mutual fund, of which there are now many, is a managed fund set up as a corporation whose sole job it is to buy and sell securities at a profit. You, the owner of stock in a mutual fund, own a share of this hypothetical corporation; thus you own a share of the mutual fund and as a co-owner you share in the profits the fund makes in the buying and selling of securities. Mutual fund stocks are quoted in the Over-the-Counter lists in financial pages of your newspaper.

There are two ways you can buy shares of mutual funds. The first is a monthly plan, where you can invest as little as $25 a month (or less, if you want to) and your money is put right to work for you at the same time that you are working toward the purchase of a share of stock of the mutual fund, much the same as it does in the Monthly Investment Plan.

A second way to buy mutual fund stock is to purchase it outright—a certain number of shares of the ABC Fund—and then to treat it just as you'd treat any other stock. You can hold it for dividends or hold it for appreciation in value, it's up to you.

The point is, your money is invested in an outfit that is professionally reinvesting your savings in the stock market with the object of earning you greater dividends and making your stock have a higher value.

The second type of mutual fund, the closed end fund or investment trust, is set up with a specified amount of capital, say, $1,000,000 and it is decided to sell 1,000,000 shares at $1.00 a share. When the money is invested in stocks profitably, the shares issued at $1.00 become worth more money, and the accumulated dividends provide more working capital with which to make more investments and so on, *ad infinitum,* provided the market remains strong and healthy.

The closed end fund grows from its original capital, so that any growth is profit. The open end fund grows from two sources: new capital coming into the fund and profit from its investment operations. No one has ever shown that one type is preferable to another.

The mutual fund is the fastest-growing financial operation in the world, and if for no other reason than that, it merits your attention.

In essence the mutual fund provides you, the small investor, with exactly the same advantages accorded the wealthy investors, and perhaps more, such as the services of professional investment managers, wide diversity, professional buying and selling "at the right time" to gain the maximum return on investments.

There is no "best" fund. Some invest only in common stocks. Some invest in highly speculative issues. Some select only stocks with growth potentials. Some stick to certain industries, like chemicals. Some seek a balance through wide diversification; others seek a balance with a mixture of stocks and bonds. Each fund, of course, has its own kind of management.

What you want in a fund will depend on what you as an individual need.

You pay for the management of your money. Usually the charge is about 8 per cent of the original purchase. Then there is also an annual management charge of ½ of 1 per cent on the value of the investment.

But for many families this is the simplest and probably the safest way to start to participate in Wall Street and the vigorous American capitalistic system.

On this factor of "safety," it is ridiculous to believe that any setup can give you complete safety for your investments. There is no such thing. If there were no risk involved, the yield on investments certainly wouldn't be very high. With a mutual fund, however, professionals keep your money as safe as possible in an auction market.

The president of one of the largest balanced mutual funds says that in addition to regular investing, diversified investing, and managed investing, a fourth ingredient is needed for the person of moderate means—*balanced investing.*

Although the investor's lot is improved substantially by investing regularly in a diversified, managed program, he needs, says this expert:

> some stable-value securities to lend stability of principal and income to the fluctuating (common stock) portion of his program. He can get this stability by "balancing" high-grade bonds and preferred stocks with the equity portion (of his investment portfolio). In short, he needs some protection against deflation as well as some hedge against inflation. A balanced program provides you with senior securities to guard against deflation and equities such as common stocks with good speculative prospects to hedge against inflation. It also eliminates the need for the investor to switch a portion of his accumulated investment fund into bonds or preferred stocks as its size increases or as the market rises.

This is a lesson in fundamental economics. If there's a depression and the prices of common stocks fall, the prices and yields of bonds and preferred stocks will remain constant. If, however, there's inflation (more likely in the remainder of the twentieth century), the prices of common stocks are likely to rise, thus protecting the value of the investments.

It is, of course, no accident that the four basic rules of investing can be satisfied by the medium of a periodic investment plan of a balanced mutual investment fund, for these plans were set up specifically to serve people wanting to accumulate funds for retirement or for other worth-while purposes.

Balanced funds can be used conveniently as the investment medium. Regular investments may be as low as $25 or $50 a month. Initially, an investment of $250 is required by many balanced funds, but this can accumulate through the monthly payments until the plan is ready to start. These regular payments are then spread over 100 to 200 or more securities which are managed by a full-time professional staff at what is, after all, a reasonable cost. A conservative balance fund, then, owning high-grade bonds and preferreds along with its common stocks, provides a complete investing program in a security.

The primary purpose of this book is to determine how long it will take a worker with average income to save some money, invest some money, and provide for his own retirement. The principal question anyone will ask is, "How old will I be when I retire?"

The table on the next page is retained because it covers a period in which securities prices as measured by all of the important averages of the day reached an all-time high, September 3, 1929. The table also covers the period of the worst depression the country has known, World War II, the reconversion period, and the start of the Korean conflict. Naturally this table cannot be used as a basis for determining future results. It does show what has happened in the past, during times when there were violent upheavals in the nation's economy.

To show how mutual funds can be made to work for you, the board chairman of a very large organization that manages several funds worked out a schedule for me showing three alternate plans for the *use* by the investor of a common stock fund.

$250 INITIAL INVESTMENT AND
$100 PER MONTH JULY 1, 1929–JANUARY 1, 1953
ALL DIVIDENDS REINVESTED AT ASSET VALUE

Year	Cumulative Payments Each Year	Total Stock Dividends from Net Income (Cumulative)	Total Cumulative Cost	Cumulative Number of Shares Owned	Cumulative Average Cost Per Share	Liquidation Value of Accumulated Shares on Dec. 31 of Each Year*
1929	$ 750	$	$ 750.00	30.807	$24.35	$ 757.24
1930	1950	55.85	2005.85	75.983	26.40	1407.96
1931	3150	171.21	3321.21	146.389	22.69	1872.32
1932	4350	383.64	4733.64	261.817	18.08	3010.90
1933	5550	575.58	6125.58	375.678	16.31	4335.32
1934	6750	850.13	7600.13	486.611	15.62	6409.32
1935	7950	1169.42	9119.42	596.069	15.30	10,031.24
1936	9150	1560.28	10,710.28	696.804	15.37	14,465.65
1937	10,350	2142.07	12,492.07	817.309	15.28	10,142.80
1938	11,550	2640.42	14,190.42	952.208	14.90	13,273.78
1939	12,750	3015.33	15,765.33	1100.967	14.32	15,875.94
1940	13,950	3565.47	17,515.47	1254.578	13.96	17,062.26
1941	15,150	4468.87	19,618.87	1422.682	13.79	17,442.08
1942	16,350	5430.97	21,780.97	1612.885	13.50	21,596.53
1943	17,550	6470.90	24,020.90	1790.805	13.41	28,133.55
1944	18,750	7576.02	26,326.02	1982.619	13.28	34,755.31
1945	19,950	8642.56	28,592.56	2200.688	12.99	44,057.77
1946	21,150	9754.67	30,904.67	2412.681	12.81	44,055.56
1947	22,350	11,203.58	33,553.58	2620.406	12.80	43,629.76
1948	23,550	12,962.98	36,512.98	2849.529	12.81	46,390.33
1949	24,750	15,257.16	40,007.16	3087.262	12.96	55,292.86
1950	25,950	17,798.65	43,748.65	3336.587	13.11	63,195.23
1951	27,150	20,502.90	47,652.90	3612.401	12.19	72,320.81
1952	28,350	23,468.12	51,818.12	3900.761	13.29	81,000.00

*Includes value of shares purchased through reinvestment of securities profits and surplus dividend of $15,433.12 during the 24-year-period.

XYZ Stock Fund, Inc.
$25 Per Month Investment Plans

TABLE I

$25 per month invested for 120 months for total of $3000.
Dividends *reinvested.*
After 10 years, i.e., starting June 1, 1972, $25 worth of shares
were redeemed monthly.

Result:

300 monthly redemption payments to owner of $25 each	$7500.00
198.654 shares balance left after the 300 monthly redemptions @ $16.132 per share asset value	3204.69
Total from original $3000 investment..........	$10,704.69

TABLE II

$25 per month invested for 120 months for total of $3000.
Dividends taken in *cash.*
After 10 years, i.e., starting June 1, 1972, $25 worth of shares
were redeemed monthly until account was completely liquidated.

Result:

129 monthly payments to owner of $25 each......	$3225.00
1 monthly payment of $7.36.................................	7.36
Total paid to owner in redemption	$3232.36
Plus dividends paid to owner in cash:	
From income..	$1544.00
From security profits	528.03
Total from original $3000 investment..........	$5304.39

TABLE III

$25 monthly invested for 120 months for total of $3000.
Dividends *reinvested.*
After 10 years, i.e., starting June 1, 1972, $50 worth of shares per

month were redeemed and cash paid to owner until account was completely liquidated.

Result:

119 monthly payments of $50 each	$5950.00
1 monthly payment of $49.50	49.50
Total from original $3000 investment..........	$5999.50

In preparing these tables we have, naturally, made certain assumptions about the future which may or may not develop. Nevertheless, we made these assumptions based on our experiences and observation of the past.

Table I shows the result of investing $25 per month for 120 months for a total of $3000, with dividends reinvested. After ten years, starting June 1, 1972, we redeemed $25 worth of shares monthly. In other words, we started to collect $25 a month from the fund.

The result is as follows:

There are 300 monthly redemption payments to the owner, of $25 each, for a total of $7500.

After payment of the 300 monthly redemption payments we get a balance of 198.645 shares of the fund worth $16.132 a share, with a total asset value of $3204.69.

Adding the redemption payments and the remaining asset value together ($7500 plus $3204.69) we get a total of $10,704.69.

Thus, Table I shows that for a $3000 investment, made over a ten-year period at the rate of $25 a month, we realized $10,-704.69. Not a bad profit!

Table II shows an investment of $25 a month for 120 months (ten years) for a total of $3000, but we took our dividends in *cash*. After ten years, starting June 1, 1972, $25 worth of shares were redeemed monthly until the account was completely liquidated.

The result is as follows:

We received 129 monthly payments as owners of the stock of $25 each for a total of $3225, plus one monthly payment of $7.36, for a total paid in redemption of $3232.36.

Dividends paid to us in cash included: from income, $1544; from security profits, $528.03.

Add them all together we received, for our original $3000 investment at $25 a month over a ten-year period, a total of $5304.39.

We made less because we had the use of our dividends as they were earned. Nevertheless, it was still a good profit.

Table III shows that we invested $25 a month for ten years, with the dividends reinvested, but after ten years, starting June 1, 1972, we redeemed $50 worth of shares a month until the account was completely liquidated.

We got 119 monthly payments of $50 each, plus one payment of $49.50, for a total of $5999.50 on our $3000 investment which we had made at $25 a month over a period of ten years.

Table II shows simply that, on paper, at least, a mutual fund will permit you to contribute $25 a month for ten years and then take out $50 a month for the next ten years, and you can come out even!

Chapter 12

Dividends: An Impressive Record

As the owner of shares of stock in a corporation, you are entitled, because of your ownership in the company, to share in the profits. These are distributed to you, usually quarterly, in the form of dividend payments.

The price of a stock—the value of a stock—is usually determined by two measures, considered jointly: its dividend rate and its prospects for the future.

It is generally conceded that a good common stock should pay a "yield" of about 6 per cent. Some, in fact many, pay more. However, some excellent common stocks pay less for the very good reason that investors, sensing something good about the future of the corporation, have bid up the price of the stock while the dividend rate has remained constant, resulting in a lower rate of yield. This does not mean that stocks with low yields are perforce "hot" and something you should buy. On the other hand, it does not mean that stocks with low yields are not good bargains.

It is recommended in this program that you permit your dividends to work for you, along with your savings. If you are in a mutual fund, you allow your dividends to accumulate. If you are handling your own investments and the dividend checks are sent to you, we recommend that you reinvest them in your regular program. This does not mean that if you are investing $25 a month or $40 a month, and you receive a dividend check for $10, you can then invest $15 of your own plus the dividend or $30 of your own plus the dividend. You are to invest $35 or $50 a month if you receive a $10 dividend. You add it to your regular program. Otherwise you're cheating yourself, and you'll feel it most and regret it most when your productive years are lost beyond recall and there's nothing you can do to remedy your mistake and petty thievery.

As a prelude to this study, officials of the New York Stock Exchange worked out a list of 662 common stocks on the Exchange that have paid cash dividends every year for 20 to 100 years.

It is an imposing list. It represents hundreds of millions of dollars paid to the owners of corporations by their hired managements in exchange for the use of their money in developing the various enterprises.

A composite of the 662 common stocks which are listed and which have paid a cash dividend in every year for 20 to 100 years would have possessed the following characteristics on April 5, 1971.

165 have paid dividends every quarter for 20 to 25 years.

103 every quarter for 25 to 30 years.

115 every quarter for 30 to 35 years.

162 every quarter for 35 to 50 years.

117 every quarter for 50 to over 100 years.

If all of these long-term dividend-payers were rolled into a single composite common stock—one share on April 5, 1971 would have cost $33⅝. Cash dividends on that share based on a median average would have totaled $1.28 in the preceding 12 months, a return of 3.8 per cent. And cash dividends, paid every three months, would have traced back to 1934.

Chapter 13

When Your Income Is Too High— the Tax Exempts

IT IS POSSIBLE TO REACH A POINT, AND I CERTAINLY HOPE IT HAPPENS to you, when your income is so high that it is unprofitable to invest in common stocks because their dividends will add so much to your income it will cost you money in taxes.

Under the tax law a single man earning more than $30,000 a year would have to own common stocks yielding something like 11 per cent in dividends to "break even" with a 3 per cent return on tax-exempt bonds.

Professional investors have taken advantage of tax-exempt bonds for years. Only recently, however, have they become popular with the smaller investors. Increasing tax burdens have been responsible for their "discovery" by the ordinary investors.

Tax-exempt bonds, called simply "tax exempts" in Wall Street, are the bonds of states and municipalities. The federal government is not allowed to tax other governments, therefore cannot collect a tax on the interest payments of state and municipal bonds.

The first and fundamental requirement of any investment is the assurance to the investor that the money he puts in will bring the largest possible return for the smallest possible risk. That's what makes these tax exempts attractive to persons in higher income tax brackets.

As investments go, municipal bonds are pleasingly "safe." There are still many tales told in Wall Street and elsewhere about the defaulting of municipal bonds during the depression. These were confined mostly to some Southern towns and to such communities that were especially hard hit financially, like Fall River, Massachusetts. However, most of the defaults have been paid up or adjusted by reducing the coupon to 2½ per cent interest for four or five years instead of the 5 or 6 per cent on the original issues, and then reverting to the original coupon when the town got back on its feet.

Today there are built-in safeguards around municipal bonds to prevent a recurrence of the defaults of the depression days, and as a result, tax-exempt states and municipals rank in safety just below securities of the United States government.

Certainly you will need the advice of experts if you are to buy tax exempts. If you buy them for their exemption feature, you will be making enough money to afford such advice.

However, somewhere along your upward climb of the ladder, you may strike a point where you decide it's more profitable for you to switch to tax-exempt bonds than it is to continue to buy common stocks.

Bonds sell in units of $1000 apiece. They are purchasable from a broker, just as common stocks are. They are quoted on the stock exchanges.

For example, if your net taxable income is $90,000 to $100,000 and you are in the 62 per cent income bracket, you would have to have a taxable bond yielding 17.11 per cent to be the equivalent of a tax-exempt bond yielding 6½ per cent.

But such benefits are not confined to the rich. A person of moderate income can likewise benefit.

If you earn $15,000 annually and are in the 25 per cent income tax bracket, you'd have to have a taxable bond yielding 8.67 per cent to give you the same profit as a tax exempt yielding 6½ per cent.

The firm of The Bond Buyer, 67 Pearl Street, New York, N.Y. 10004, compiled a table of taxable equivalent yields related to each income bracket. It makes interesting reading if you'll look up your own bracket and make the comparison.

TAXABLE EQUIVALENT YIELDS
INDIVIDUAL INCOME BRACKETS—THOUSANDS OF DOLLARS

SINGLE RETURN		$12 to $14	$14 to $16		$16 to $18	$18 to $20	$20 to $22		$22 to $26		$26 to $32
JOINT RETURN	$16 to $20			$20 to $24		$24 to $28		$28 to $32		$32 to $36	$36 to $40
% Tax	28%	29%	31%	32%	34%	36%	38%	39%	40%	42%	45%
TAX EXEMPT YIELDS											
2.50	3.47	3.52	3.62	3.68	3.79	3.91	4.03	4.10	4.17	4.31	4.55
3.00	4.17	4.23	4.35	4.41	4.55	4.69	4.84	4.92	5.00	5.17	5.45
3.25	4.51	4.58	4.71	4.78	4.92	5.08	5.24	5.33	5.42	5.60	5.91
3.50	4.86	4.93	5.07	5.15	5.30	5.47	5.65	5.74	5.83	6.03	6.36
3.75	5.21	5.28	5.43	5.51	5.68	5.86	6.05	6.15	6.25	6.47	6.82
4.00	5.56	5.63	5.80	5.88	6.06	6.25	6.45	6.56	6.67	6.90	7.27
4.10	5.69	5.77	5.94	6.03	6.21	6.41	6.61	6.72	6.83	7.07	7.45
4.20	5.83	5.92	6.09	6.18	6.36	6.56	6.77	6.89	7.00	7.24	7.64
4.25	5.90	5.99	6.16	6.25	6.44	6.64	6.85	6.97	7.08	7.33	7.73
4.30	5.97	6.06	6.23	6.32	6.52	6.72	6.94	7.05	7.17	7.41	7.82
4.40	6.11	6.20	6.38	6.47	6.67	6.87	7.10	7.21	7.33	7.59	8.00
4.50	6.25	6.34	6.52	6.62	6.82	7.03	7.26	7.38	7.50	7.76	8.18
4.60	6.39	6.48	6.67	6.76	6.97	7.19	7.42	7.54	7.67	7.93	8.36
4.70	6.53	6.62	6.81	6.91	7.12	7.34	7.58	7.70	7.83	8.10	8.55
4.75	6.60	6.69	6.88	6.99	7.20	7.42	7.66	7.79	7.92	8.19	8.64
4.80	6.67	6.76	6.96	7.06	7.27	7.50	7.74	7.87	8.00	8.28	8.73
4.90	6.81	6.90	7.10	7.21	7.42	7.66	7.90	8.03	8.17	8.45	8.91
5.00	6.94	7.04	7.25	7.35	7.58	7.81	8.06	8.20	8.33	8.62	9.09
5.10	7.08	7.18	7.39	7.50	7.73	7.97	8.23	8.36	8.50	8.79	9.27
5.20	7.22	7.32	7.54	7.65	7.88	8.12	8.39	8.52	8.67	8.97	9.45
5.25	7.29	7.39	7.61	7.72	7.95	8.20	8.47	8.61	8.75	9.05	9.55
5.30	7.36	7.46	7.68	7.79	8.03	8.28	8.55	8.69	8.83	9.14	9.64
5.40	7.50	7.61	7.83	7.94	8.18	8.44	8.71	8.85	9.00	9.31	9.82
5.50	7.64	7.75	7.97	8.09	8.33	8.59	8.87	9.02	9.17	9.48	10.00
5.60	7.78	7.89	8.12	8.24	8.48	8.75	9.03	9.18	9.33	9.66	10.18
5.70	7.92	8.03	8.26	8.38	8.64	8.91	9.19	9.34	9.50	9.83	10.36
5.75	7.99	8.10	8.33	8.46	8.71	8.98	9.27	9.43	9.58	9.91	10.45
5.80	8.06	8.17	8.41	8.53	8.79	9.06	9.35	9.51	9.67	10.00	10.55
5.90	8.19	8.31	8.55	8.68	8.94	9.22	9.52	9.67	9.83	10.17	10.73
6.00	8.33	8.45	8.70	8.82	9.09	9.37	9.68	9.84	10.00	10.34	10.91
6.10	8.47	8.59	8.84	8.97	9.24	9.53	9.84	10.00	10.17	10.52	11.09
6.20	8.61	8.73	8.99	9.12	9.39	9.69	10.00	10.16	10.33	10.69	11.27
6.25	8.68	8.80	9.06	9.19	9.47	9.77	10.08	10.25	10.42	10.78	11.36
6.30	8.75	8.87	9.13	9.26	9.55	9.84	10.16	10.33	10.50	10.86	11.45
6.40	8.89	9.01	9.28	9.41	9.70	10.00	10.32	10.49	10.67	11.03	11.64
6.50	9.03	9.15	9.42	9.56	9.85	10.16	10.48	10.66	10.83	11.21	11.82
6.60	9.17	9.30	9.57	9.71	10.00	10.31	10.65	10.82	11.00	11.38	12.00
6.70	9.31	9.44	9.71	9.85	10.15	10.47	10.81	10.98	11.17	11.55	12.18
6.75	9.37	9.51	9.78	9.93	10.23	10.55	10.89	11.07	11.25	11.64	12.27
6.80	9.44	9.58	9.86	10.00	10.30	10.62	10.97	11.15	11.33	11.72	12.36
6.90	9.58	9.72	10.00	10.15	10.45	10.78	11.13	11.31	11.50	11.90	12.55
7.00	9.72	9.86	10.14	10.29	10.61	10.94	11.29	11.48	11.67	12.07	12.73
7.10	9.86	10.00	10.29	10.44	10.76	11.09	11.45	11.64	11.83	12.24	12.91
7.20	10.00	10.14	10.43	10.59	10.91	11.25	11.61	11.80	12.00	12.41	13.09
7.25	10.07	10.21	10.51	10.66	10.98	11.33	11.69	11.89	12.08	12.50	13.18
7.30	10.14	10.28	10.58	10.74	11.06	11.41	11.77	11.97	12.17	12.59	13.27
7.40	10.28	10.42	10.72	10.88	11.21	11.56	11.94	12.13	12.33	12.76	13.45
7.50	10.42	10.56	10.87	11.03	11.36	11.72	12.10	12.30	12.50	12.93	13.64
7.75	10.76	10.92	11.23	11.40	11.74	12.11	12.50	12.70	12.92	13.36	14.09
8.00	11.11	11.27	11.59	11.76	12.12	12.50	12.90	13.11	13.33	13.79	14.55
8.25	11.46	11.62	11.96	12.13	12.50	12.89	13.31	13.52	13.75	14.22	15.00
8.50	11.81	11.97	12.32	12.50	12.88	13.28	13.71	13.93	14.17	14.66	15.45
8.75	12.15	12.32	12.68	12.87	13.26	13.67	14.11	14.34	14.58	15.09	15.91
9.00	12.50	12.68	13.04	13.24	13.64	14.06	14.52	14.75	15.00	15.52	16.36

TAXABLE EQUIVALENT YIELDS
INDIVIDUAL INCOME BRACKETS—THOUSANDS OF DOLLARS

	$32 to $38		$38 to $44		$44 to $50	$50 to $60	$60 to $70	$70 to $80	$80 to $90	$90 to $100	over $100
$40 to $44	$44 to $52	$52 to $64	$64 to $76	$76 to $88	$88 to $100	$100 to $120	$120 to $140	$140 to $160	$160 to $180	$180 to $200	over $200
48%	50%	53%	55%	58%	60%	62%	64%	66%	68%	69%	70%
4.81	5.00	5.32	5.56	5.95	6.25	6.58	6.94	7.35	7.81	8.06	8.33
5.77	6.00	6.38	6.67	7.14	7.50	7.89	8.33	8.82	9.38	9.68	10.00
6.25	6.50	6.91	7.22	7.74	8.13	8.55	9.03	9.56	10.16	10.48	10.83
6.73	7.00	7.45	7.78	8.33	8.75	9.21	9.72	10.29	10.94	11.29	11.67
7.21	7.50	7.98	8.33	8.93	9.38	9.87	10.42	11.03	11.72	12.10	12.50
7.69	8.00	8.51	8.89	9.52	10.00	10.53	11.11	11.76	12.50	12.90	13.33
7.88	8.20	8.72	9.11	9.76	10.25	10.79	11.39	12.06	12.81	13.23	13.67
8.08	8.40	8.94	9.33	10.00	10.50	11.05	11.67	12.35	13.12	13.55	14.00
8.17	8.50	9.04	9.44	10.12	10.63	11.18	11.81	12.50	13.28	13.71	14.17
8.27	8.60	9.15	9.56	10.24	10.75	11.32	11.94	12.65	13.44	13.87	14.33
8.46	8.80	9.36	9.78	10.48	11.00	11.58	12.22	12.94	13.75	14.19	14.67
8.65	9.00	9.57	10.00	10.71	11.25	11.84	12.50	13.24	14.06	14.52	15.00
8.85	9.20	9.79	10.22	10.95	11.50	12.11	12.78	13.53	14.38	14.84	15.33
9.04	9.40	10.00	10.44	11.19	11.75	12.37	13.06	13.82	14.69	15.16	15.67
9.13	9.50	10.11	10.56	11.31	11.88	12.50	13.19	13.97	14.84	15.32	15.83
9.23	9.60	10.21	10.67	11.43	12.00	12.63	13.33	14.12	15.00	15.48	16.00
9.42	9.80	10.43	10.89	11.67	12.25	12.89	13.61	14.41	15.31	15.81	16.33
9.62	10.00	10.64	11.11	11.90	12.50	13.16	13.89	14.71	15.63	16.13	16.67
9.81	10.20	10.85	11.33	12.14	12.75	13.42	14.17	15.00	15.94	16.45	17.00
10.00	10.40	11.06	11.56	12.38	13.00	13.68	14.44	15.29	16.25	16.77	17.33
10.10	10.50	11.17	11.67	12.50	13.12	13.82	14.58	15.44	16.41	16.94	17.50
10.19	10.60	11.28	11.78	12.62	13.25	13.95	14.72	15.59	16.56	17.10	17.67
10.38	10.80	11.49	12.00	12.86	13.50	14.21	15.00	15.88	16.87	17.42	18.00
10.58	11.00	11.70	12.22	13.10	13.75	14.47	15.28	16.18	17.19	17.74	18.33
10.77	11.20	11.91	12.44	13.33	14.00	14.74	15.56	16.47	17.50	18.06	18.67
10.96	11.40	12.13	12.67	13.57	14.25	15.00	15.83	16.76	17.81	18.39	19.00
11.06	11.50	12.23	12.78	13.69	14.38	15.13	15.97	16.91	17.97	18.55	19.17
11.15	11.60	12.34	12.89	13.81	14.50	15.26	16.11	17.06	18.13	18.71	19.33
11.35	11.80	12.55	13.11	14.05	14.75	15.53	16.39	17.35	18.44	19.03	19.67
11.54	12.00	12.77	13.33	14.29	15.00	15.79	16.67	17.65	18.75	19.35	20.00
11.73	12.20	12.98	13.56	14.52	15.25	16.05	16.94	17.94	19.06	19.68	20.33
11.92	12.40	13.19	13.78	14.76	15.50	16.32	17.22	18.24	19.37	20.00	20.67
12.02	12.50	13.30	13.89	14.88	15.63	16.45	17.36	18.38	19.53	20.16	20.83
12.12	12.60	13.40	14.00	15.00	15.75	16.58	17.50	18.53	19.69	20.32	21.00
12.31	12.80	13.62	14.22	15.24	16.00	16.84	17.78	18.82	20.00	20.65	21.33
12.50	13.00	13.83	14.44	15.48	16.25	17.11	18.06	19.12	20.31	20.97	21.67
12.69	13.20	14.04	14.67	15.71	16.50	17.37	18.33	19.41	20.63	21.29	22.00
12.88	13.40	14.26	14.89	15.95	16.75	17.63	18.61	19.71	20.94	21.61	22.33
12.98	13.50	14.36	15.00	16.07	16.87	17.76	18.75	19.85	21.09	21.77	22.50
13.08	13.60	14.47	15.11	16.19	17.00	17.89	18.89	20.00	21.25	21.94	22.67
13.27	13.80	14.68	15.33	16.43	17.25	18.16	19.17	20.29	21.56	22.26	23.00
13.46	14.00	14.89	15.56	16.67	17.50	18.42	19.44	20.59	21.88	22.58	23.33
13.65	14.20	15.11	15.78	16.90	17.75	18.68	19.72	20.88	22.19	22.90	23.67
13.85	14.40	15.32	16.00	17.14	18.00	18.95	20.00	21.18	22.50	23.23	24.00
13.94	14.50	15.43	16.11	17.26	18.13	19.08	20.14	21.32	22.66	23.39	24.17
14.04	14.60	15.53	16.22	17.38	18.25	19.21	20.28	21.47	22.81	23.55	24.33
14.23	14.80	15.74	16.44	17.62	18.50	19.47	20.56	21.76	23.13	23.87	24.67
14.42	15.00	15.96	16.67	17.86	18.75	19.74	20.83	22.06	23.44	24.19	25.00
14.90	15.50	16.49	17.22	18.45	19.37	20.39	21.53	22.79	24.22	25.00	25.83
15.38	16.00	17.02	17.78	19.05	20.00	21.05	22.22	23.53	25.00	25.81	26.67
15.87	16.50	17.55	18.33	19.64	20.63	21.71	22.92	24.26	25.78	26.61	27.50
16.35	17.00	18.09	18.89	20.24	21.25	22.37	23.61	25.00	26.56	27.42	28.33
16.83	17.50	18.62	19.44	20.83	21.87	23.03	24.31	25.74	27.34	28.23	29.17
17.31	18.00	19.15	20.00	21.43	22.50	23.68	25.00	26.47	28.12	29.03	30.00

Part III

And Retire

Chapter 14

How Old Must You Be to Retire?

IF YOU WANT TO RETIRE SOONER, IT MAY NOT BE NECESSARY TO PLOD those interminable years until you're entitled to some kind of pension and/or Social Security. If you so desire, perhaps you can retire many years before that magic age of sixty-five.

There have been many times when every man, watching his children grow up into strangers and witnessing the fading of his wife's bloom and the erosion of his own youth and vitality, has cried out against the system which provides him with leisure in his twilight years when many of the important things of his life have passed him by or withered, and which demands all of his time and energy when he should be enjoying life to the full.

We find ourselves enslaved to a career, at least to a job, when our children and our wives need us most. Many a man has retired at sixty-five only to discover that his children have lives of their own and no longer need him and that his wife, throughout the years, has built a life of her own and that she operates in a separate solar system, just a little bit removed from his own.

Retirement to such a couple may be fun because it's a new phase of life, albeit the final one. But it's not a fruitful phase.

Is there anything more abject than a lonely and wistful old man sitting resigned and introspective in the sun while the world speeds on around him, ignoring him in his solitary retirement and impatient of his wistful memories of the times when he, too, took part in Operation Make-the-World-Go-Round?

What's more pitiful, really, than the incessantly bridge-playing, idle-retired, and idle-rich of St. Petersburg, eagerly seeking to fill their hours with the artificial stimulus of a game of cards lest the greatest hazard of idleness, boredom, seize them in its grasp and render them victims of the most miserable malady of the aged and aging?

The two greatest mistakes made by those about to retire are these: *1.* To suppose that money alone can provide a comfortable retirement, and *2.* To suppose that a wide variety of interests and aptitudes alone can make a person capable of enjoying a happy retirement.

It takes both money and interests to be able to retire. Not until you possess *both* can you successfully quit your job and start life anew.

But when you do have both money and the know-how of retirement, you're ready for that big step, whether you're thirty-five or sixty-five.

So when is the earliest you can retire? When you're fully prepared, both financially and morally; when you can support yourself with the money you have accumulated; and when you are equipped to lead a full and relatively active life doing the things you *want* to do rather than the things you've been *forced* to do to earn a living.

You should not retire until you're ready, on both these counts. If you have the money at age sixty-five but have no idea of what you're going to do with your time when you've retired, then you should keep on working.

Preparing for retirement is like preparing for a career. It's as distinct a part of life these days as the three previous phases: the working years, the school years, and the childhood years. We would not think of permitting children to grow up without incessant instructions about human behavior. In our school years we prepare for the careers of our working years.

Thus it follows logically that during the course of our working years we should be preparing for the next step: retirement.

We should no sooner begin our retirement without adequate preparation than we would begin a career without education; for an unprepared-for retirement, like an unplanned-for career, is doomed.

If you have always wanted to breed chinchillas, build ships in bottles, sail boats around Cape Horn, or become a serious naturalist photographer, but have been prevented from doing so by lack of time, you should plan now, whatever your age, for the fulfillment of your dreams in your retirement, when freedom from responsibility and a time schedule will permit you to do it.

As you prepare your finances, you should also prepare your retirement "career."

I know a merchandise buyer who spent twenty years "dabbling" in amateur photography. Three or four years before his retirement he began to submit prints in some of the national photographic contests and succeeded, finally, in winning an honorable mention.

After retirement, however, he pursued his hobby almost as he would a career and thus far has accumulated several cash prizes and has sold "spreads" to some of the big national picture magazines.

Yet he's free—free to come and go as he pleases, and to lie abed until noon if he wishes, and moreover, if he doesn't *feel* like taking pictures he doesn't have to, for his income is assured from his retirement fund.

That, I submit, is *living.*

This friend will never have to fill his days with bridge and his evenings with vodka-and-tonics to prevent being overwhelmed with boredom. He was ready for retirement as soon as his bankroll was.

The point I wish to make is this: I can show you the easiest way to save your money and the logical way to invest it so that you can *afford* to retire at almost any age of your choice. But no second party can show you how to do the equally important part, the building of your retirement career.

Chapter 15

How to Finance Your Retirement

YOU MAY NOT REALIZE IT WHEN YOU HAVE ENOUGH MONEY TO RETIRE. Many persons are working today who, if they but took an accounting of their resources, would soon recognize the fact that they could have retired months, even years, ago.

You will have enough money for retirement when:

1. You can take the cash-surrender value of a good portion of your life insurance and add it to your investments.

2. Your savings account is sufficient to handle any emergencies.

3. Your investment in your house is sufficient to buy you a smaller, less expensive place and will permit adding a substantial amount to your investment portfolio.

4. Your investments, with the cashed-in portion of your life insurance and the equity of your house added, will yield you a sufficient, safe income.

In time, if you qualify, you can count on the benefits of your Social Security program as well.

It depends what you're willing to settle for in retirement, how well you want to live.

How much money should you leave in your savings account? I'd say enough to take care of unforeseen expenses.

How much money should you leave in your insurance program? I'd say $5000 worth of paid-up life insurance, for all you really want now is enough money for final expenses.

If after the sale of your home and the purchase of a less-expensive and smaller "retirement" home, you have sufficient money to provide you the income you need to live on, then I'd say you're financially ready for retirement.

Here's a personal equation to consider:

If at the age of forty-eight, a man cashes in all but $5000 paid-up life insurance, has $10,000 in the bank, has bought and paid for a retirement home, and still has, with cashed-in insurance, savings (besides the $10,000 emergency fund) and investments, a total of $100,000 he should be able to retire.

With the $100,000 invested in good securities he can be reasonably assured of an $8000 annual income, for $8000 is 8 per cent of $100,000 and a portfolio of good securities should yield at least 8 per cent.

If he's willing to settle on an $8000 annual income he can retire with reasonable confidence at age forty-eight, for even if his investments *do not* yield him 8 per cent, he can get by. If they yield absolutely nothing, he can take $8000 per year out of his capital for fourteen years before he exhausts it, bringing him up to age sixty-two when he'll be entitled to Social Security.

In this exercise we assume that an investment portfolio consisting of a man's life savings is not going to depreciate in value. In the first two sections of this book, in *Save It,* and in *Invest It,* I have explained why I do not believe that over the long haul, the stock market is going to go into any notable tailspin. Furthermore, with $100,000 to invest, it should be possible to get such a wide diversity of stocks to protect against losses, even if the market softens for an abnormally long period.

With planned savings, with a planned, *heavy* insurance program, and with wise investing, it is not difficult for an ordinary fellow with an ordinary career and ordinary income to accumulate a net worth of $100,000 by the age of forty-eight, if he starts early enough.

There is no mathematical formula that can be applied. There is no schedule that can be set up saying that if a man of twenty-five years of age earns a certain amount of money each year he can, by the age of forty-eight, have a net worth of $100,000 plus paid-up insurance of $5000, plus a savings account of $10,000, plus a paid-for home.

But he *can* do it, as logic will tell you. He can do it if he wants to.

Throughout the years you should have periodic review of your stock holdings. This is essential. Stocks which several years ago appeared to have a promising future may no longer seem attractive; and it is only common sense to have your portfolio checked over once or twice a year, and to replace stocks having no better than average prospects with stocks whose future is brighter.

But when it comes to retirement, do nothing capriciously with your investments, for they're what you're going to live on for the rest of your life.

When retirement comes, *income* is more important in stocks than growth prospects and it might be more profitable, or more sensible, to replace some of your common stocks in the portfolio with higher-yielding common or preferred stocks. You might also want to get into some tax exempts.

Combined, your income will have to be sufficient to provide you with a moderately active life. How big your capital investment has to be depends on how actively you want to live after retirement. A fellow who wants to maintain his yacht, or even his cabin cruiser, in his retirement years, may find that his total capital investment will have to be larger than the fellow's who intends to live in a small home in South Carolina and pursue a hobby of painting in oils.

Only you can decide when the magic point has been reached,

for only you will know how much retirement income you will need, and only you will be able to tell how much you can expect from your investments.

If your investments are all in securites you should expect a minimum of the current average yield. If there's less yield there's something wrong with your portfolio and you should seek advice. At any rate, no matter what move you make with your portfolio, you should do so only with competent help.

At some point along the way you may decide you're fed up with the whims and caprices of the stock market and the people in it, and you may want someone else to manage your money for you in your old age. You may sell your securities and buy some insurance annuities outright. Or you may decide to buy some mutual-fund shares outright.

The point is, if you've handled your program well, you'll have money enough to do about as you wish.

How much money have you "saved" in your insurance program? Get out your policies and check the cash-surrender value in them.

Then look ahead to the age you expect to retire. By retirement age you won't need all the insurance protection you're buying now. You and your wife won't face so many years alone if either of you dies. Your home will be paid for, your children grown. There'll be income from securities and possibly from Social Security. The insurance money your wife will need will be primarily for final expenses and for any expensive medical care.

You can, at retirement age, cash in most of your insurance, leaving a relatively small amount of $10,000 or $5000. Thus you will have *used* your insurance through life. It will have afforded you maximum protection when you needed it most, when your wife faced many years of potential widowhood if anything had happened to you, and when your children were expensively growing up in a world with a price tag on nearly everything.

And at retirement age your insurance miraculously changes

into accumulated savings, to permit you to live out your life with freedom and independence. Thus, if I may be permitted to call myself expert in matters of personal finance, I'd say that in a society that is financially complex and sometimes mysterious, life insurance is probably the best bargain you'll ever find.

How does a man of moderate means *save* enough and *invest* enough so that he can retire comfortably without an anxiety-filled old age?

There's no easy road to retirement and independence. If it were easy, it wouldn't be as desirable as it appears to you now.

But . . .

You have learned that *saving* isn't as difficult as it may have seemed.

You have learned that *investing* wisely isn't an impossible accomplishment.

Your willingness to save and your ability to invest can, if you permit them, make it possible for you to retire.

With the help of the actuarial department of the Mutual Life Insurance Company of New York, I have dug up some theoretical figures, which, if applied, must have been *actual* figures. They concern the life of one Henry P. Bluechip, a character of spontaneous invention, but a lad who might have existed nevertheless. He was of a previous generation, but his story is still interesting.

When Henry was married at the age of twenty-two, he embarked on a rigid savings program. Then he took out a $10,000 life insurance policy of the kind called ordinary life or whole-life. It cost him, at that age, $154.70 a year.

Henry was making $50 a week, or $2600 a year at the time.

He and his bride, Mary E. Bluechip, had decided that since their commitments were moderate, they could easily afford to save 20 per cent, or $10 a week, which would equal $520 a year.

Since the life insurance cost only $154.70 a year, they put the balance of the $520 in a "must" savings account, or to be specific, they saved $365.30 a year. This they did at the rate of $7.00 a week (divide fifty-two weeks into $365.30).

When our friend Henry Bluechip was twenty-five years old, he purchased another $10,000 worth of life insurance. Since he was three years older, it cost him $168.20 a year. Ten years went by and he had progressed well in his job when he bought his third $10,000 policy at a cost of $228.70 a year. He was then thirty-five. At the age of forty, nearing the peak of his earning capacity, he bought another $10,000 worth of insurance at a cost of $271.30 a year.

In all, Henry had $40,000 worth of insurance by age fifty, and he arranged to pay a few dollars extra each year to give himself double-indemnity coverage. This meant that if he was killed in some mishap, his wife would get double his coverage, or $80,-000. After all, Henry reasoned, if he was to die before his time, it would be more likely because of some accident than as a result of disease.

(Henry actually bought an "executive modified life policy" offered by a prominent mutual life insurance company and his premiums during the first three years were lower than the average premium of the policy throughout his life. For instance, the policy he bought at the age of twenty-two started out costing $154.70, but in the fourth year of the policy's life the cost increased to $171.50. Similar ratios maintained for the other three policies: at twenty-five, $168.20 for three years, then $186.90 yearly from then on; age thirty-five, $228.70 for three years, then $254.10; at age forty, $271.30 for three years, then $301.40.)

At age forty-four, Henry was spending $914.30 a year for insurance coverage. But Henry, at age forty-four, was earning $12,000, which meant that he still had to bank some money in a savings account in order to adhere to his program of "thrift for retirement."

It gave him a wonderful feeling of security, for he knew that if anything happened to him, Mary would be well cared for because of his insurance money, and he also knew that if nothing happened to him he in due time would be well cared for, since to Henry insurance wasn't something to collect only when you die; it was part of his savings program—a wonderful device that permitted him to save while it protected his wife and children against any hardship, foreseeable or unforeseeable.

On his sixtieth birthday Henry Bluechip and his wife Mary took a trip to Florida, their first. Henry saw bone fishing for the first time in his life, and fell in love with the sport. He had always been an ardent fisherman, though he had always confined his sport to the coastal waters of New England or the inland fresh lakes of the region. Bone fishing and the hunting of marlin and barracuda excited him beyond any sport he had ever before witnessed.

When Henry and Mary returned home from their Florida vacation, Henry felt restless, dissatisfied with his job. He fretted that a whole year would have to elapse before he could return to Florida to pursue the sport that had become a major love in his life.

One night Henry broached the subject of retirement tentatively.

"Good heavens!" Mary exclaimed. "We could never afford it. You won't get a pension until you're sixty-five. You know that your company pension plan is tied in with your Social Security."

"But Mary," her husband protested, "we've *saved* a great deal of money. We certainly have enough to provide us with five years of living until my pension and Social Security come due."

"Yes, but you'll have to settle for less pension if you quit now," Mary reminded him.

But the lust for bone fishing persisted and Henry sat down at his desk to figure out the status of his finances.

He tackled his insurance first. Fortunately he had permitted his dividends to accumulate and be reinvested for him by the insurance company. That gave him a higher guaranteed cash-surrender value in each policy.

The policy he bought when he was twenty-two years old had a cash-surrender value of $8960.

The policy he bought when he was twenty-five years old had a cash-surrender value of $8530.

The policy he bought when he was thirty-five years old had a cash-surrender value of $6910.

The policy he bought when he was forty years old had a cash-surrender value of $5920.

If he cashed in on all his insurance, Henry would get a check for $30,320!

He also had $1500 in savings in the bank.

He had $11,000 worth of securities in a portfolio he had been "building up" for years with savings-converted-to-stocks.

He also had a $25,000 home that he owned free and clear.

Henry added it up, blinked, and totaled the figures again. He could hardly believe it!

Why, he was worth:

$67,820!

And he had always considered himself a poor man!

Henry scribbled rapidly now, the excitement of discovery and of hope surging through his veins.

He decided he would have to leave the $1500 in the savings account.

And he'd better buy a $3000 paid-up life insurance policy which would, through the years until his death, swell with interest and accumulated dividends.

That left him:

$27,320 in cash from his insurance
$11,000 worth of stocks
$25,000 equity in his home.

His retirement fund was:

$63,320!

He had no idea he had accumulated so much wealth.

Let's see, he figured, he'd have to buy a home in Florida. One he and Mary had priced with two bedrooms—plenty of room for the two of them, now that the kids were grown and married—cost $12,500.

That left more than $50,000 to retire on!

He hurried to Mary with the figures. Mary was impressed. From what they knew of the stock market, they were confident they could get at least 6 per cent a year on a $50,000 portfolio. At least they'd have $3000 income, which they calculated was plenty for them since their tastes were simple and their needs moderate.

And in five years the pension would start—a smaller one than they had been expecting but sufficient to make a good, stable foundation for their retirement comfort.

So Henry Bluechip retired and he and Mary moved to Florida in a $12,500 home where they lived happily ever after.

Henry cheated a little and made a slight capital investment in addition to the new home. He bought a boat worth $2500. But he and Mary are about the most ardent bone fishermen on the Atlantic Coast. Both are sunbrowned and hale, though by this time he's been collecting Social Security for years.

A fairy story?

In Henry's case, yes. But it needn't be in yours.

Remember these facts about Henry!

He started from scratch—he made his own way, *all* the way.

Henry never earned more than $12,000 a year in his life.

He saved it.

He invested it.

Then he retired, and he didn't have to *depend* on his company pension or his Social Security. Henry was beholden to no one.

Truly, Henry was—and still is—captain of his own soul.

Henry need not be envied.

He can be emulated.

If Henry's insurance figures confuse you, and you'd like to compare them with your own policies, here's a breakdown of how they worked. (Extras, such as double indemnity, are not included.)

EXECUTIVE MODIFIED LIFE POLICY
Issued in minimum amounts of $10,000

	Age 22	*Age 25*	*Age 35*	*Age 40*
ANNUAL PREMIUM				
(Per thousand dollars)				
First three years	$15.47	$16.82	$22.87	$27.13
Fourth year and later	17.19	18.69	25.41	30.14
CASH-SURRENDER VALUE				
AT AGE 60				
Guaranteed	$554	$538	$463	$411
With accumulated				
dividends	896	953	691	592
(estimated)				
Average net annual cost				
over a 20-year period				
with accumulated				
dividends	$13.08	$14.14	$18.95	$22.49

Henry also might have taken out the flexible life policies which are paid up in full at the age of ninety.

The breakdown on this kind of policy would have worked out:

FLEXIBLE LIFE POLICY
(paid up at age 90)
Issued in minimum amounts of $5000

	Age 22	*Age 25*	*Age 35*	*Age 40*
ANNUAL PREMIUM				
(Per thousand dollars)				
	$17.88	$19.40	$26.17	$30.92

CASH-SURRENDER VALUE
     AT AGE 60
     Guaranteed $557 $540 $467 $416
     With accumulated
          dividends (estimated) $901 $857 $695 $595

Average net annual cost
     over a 20-year period $14.08 $15.18 $20.13 $23.77

Chapter 16

Investments After Retirement

WHEN YOU HAVE SOLD YOUR HOME AND CASHED IN MOST OF YOUR life insurance and have toted up what you have managed to save, you will need to invest in something that will yield you at least 6 per cent, and more, if possible. Thus, if you're planning to earn $600 a year on each $10,000 of investment, you're going to need $50,000 worth of investment capital if you decide that you and your wife will require $3000 a year in addition to Social Security and your company pension plan, if any, in order to live comfortably.

That is, incidentally, a minimum retirement income if you own your own retirement home, start out with good furnishings, adequate wardrobes, and most of the essentials and luxuries you'll need and particularly if you have, in addition, some source of supplemental income which can be realized by occasional, casual, or intermittent work.

You might make more on your investment in a business which requires some casual work from you in addition to some capital. You may, by looking around, find just the kind of business you'd like to own, one that needs only part-time work from you and yet yields substantially more than 6 per cent on your investment.

It's up to you.

But if you're an average fellow, you'll invest your capital in securities and let someone else work for you. If you do, you're *entitled* to at least 6 per cent before taxes on your investment.

At the preliminary stage of your retirement everything that you have accumulated may be regarded as "savings," all your insurance, all your cash-in-bank, all of the equity in your real estate, and all of your investments.

Just what you do with this accumulation of wealth—and its size should surprise you as much as it surprised Henry Blue-chip—depends on two things: *1.* How much you've saved; and *2.* How much you'll need in retirement income.

You will have to use your own judgment.

If, for instance, you have managed to gather together $100,-000 and you decide you too can get along on $6000 annual retirement income, you'd be silly to do anything but buy annuities paying 6 per cent or bonds (government, good corporate, or good tax exempts) paying 6 per cent or more.

Or you might decide to give yourself a guaranteed income of $3000 with $50,000 worth of annuities and an additional $3000 income with $50,000 in good securities paying at least 6 per cent.

Do such delightful problems seem remote to you? They needn't be, not if you play your cards properly.

Everything depends on how much you'll need. You'll have to work out a budget and be prepared to stick to it. It will have to be a good budget, too, for after retirement you won't be able to go to the boss and pressure for another raise. You'll be living with a more or less rigid income for the remainder of your life.

In a previous book, *Teach Your Wife to Be a Widow,* I recommended three different portfolios of investments for widows, one for $10,000, one for $25,000, and a third for $50,000. The $10,000 portfolio had a yield of 6.18 per cent; the $25,000 a yield of 6.14 per cent; and the $50,000 a yield of 5.96 per cent. In the years since those portfolios were drawn up, in 1951, the stocks in them have appreciated greatly, with the result that the $25,-000 investment, for instance, would be worth twice again as much today and the yield, accordingly, would be greater.

Today, being older and presumably wiser, and knowing something more about Wall Street and, I hope, about the nation's economy, I would hesitate to recommend any specific investments in even a "typical" portfolio. For one thing, a portfolio, like anything else, has a limited life. It must be changed as the economy changes, as people's spending habits change.

A person with $50,000 might want to take the whole amount and buy the shares of a good mutual fund whose history, over a significant period, has shown that the fund has a consistent ability to produce at least 6 per cent in dividends per year. This might be a reasonably easy solution to an investment problem.

However, if you've been doing your own investing through the years you should be able to continue doing it after you have retired. There's only one difference, but it's a major difference: *In retirement you cannot afford many losses.* You'll have no other income to help you replace any money you lose from capital.

You should trade your securities only on competent, professional advice. You will have learned, by retirement age, that when it comes to brokers, advisers are legion, but the competent comprise but a small squad.

You will need protection and security in your investments. This means that you will buy fair amounts of high-grade securities and you will *diversify*. By high-grade securities I do not, perforce, mean blue chips. Neither do I imply here that blue chips should be avoided. Balance is what you're after in a retirement portfolio, balance and protection.

As a retired person you'll not be trying to amass more capital, hence you'll not be looking particularly for growth stocks, those which are low-priced now but are destined, for one reason or another, to be worth more in the future.

Instead you'll be looking for those stocks with excellent histories and with regular—and foreseeably regular—dividend records. In short, you're seeking a refuge for your hard-earned capital which will not only assure it of safekeeping but will, as well, produce a reasonably high, reasonably secure, and a reasonably steady income.

Such stocks exist.

If they did not, trust companies could not manage trust funds, mutual funds could not exist without painful and costly policing, and insurance companies would not be willing to sign a contract for annuities.

You can find out which stocks these are by consulting a well-regarded brokerage firm.

Buy for diversity—and see that you diversify by type of issue, industry and company.

Perhaps you should not buy stocks exclusively. Perhaps you should buy bonds as well, or some other kind of fixed-income investments. Your broker, if he's a good one, will advise you carefully on this point. Insist that he do so.

Once your program has been set up, once you and your broker have selected a portfolio, it might be wiser to more or less forget it except for certain twice-yearly periods. You can keep an eye on your securities by reading the financial pages of your newspaper, but do not, in retirement, read the stock list apprehensively. All stocks, even the best, move higher and lower in moderate fluctuations. In retirement, you're interested in dividends, not in price of security, unless there's a drastic fluctuation in a particular stock.

Twice a year review the portfolio with the broker whom you have selected for his understanding, patience, and competence.

The big mistake most retired persons make is in trying to *make money* with their retirement capital. The habits of a lifetime are hard to shake, and certainly, up to the point of retirement, anyone is expected to make as much money from his investments as possible. But the biggest rewards frequently come from the greatest risks, and that's a luxury you cannot indulge or afford once you've been guest of honor at that office farewell party. Your days of speculation are over then.

But it's a mistake to worry over your capital.

If you retire at age sixty with $50,000 as Henry Bluechip did in Chapter 15, you don't have to maintain a capital account of $50,000 until the day you die. That is, you don't unless you particularly want to make it especially easy for your children. Each year, if you'll face the fact frankly, diminishes your need for total capital.

If at the age of eighty-five you decide to dip into your capital fund by $5000 a year for a gala fling at life, you're not running much risk of an impoverished old age. The fact is, if you want to be truthful about it, it's more sensible for you to enjoy the money than it is to leave it to some relatives, no matter how dear they are to you, because the relatives should, under nominal conditions, be making their own way, just as you did.

Thus, the most important thing facing you when you begin your retirement—security—is something you'll need in diminishing value as your retirement progresses and as you near, as all men do, the end of the road.

At the outset of your retirement you'll need maximum safety in your investments. Later on this should concern you less and less unless you've developed some powerful hormone to warrant abnormal expectations of longevity.

The only reason you'll be retiring is because you want to enjoy life. You won't be quitting because you're lazy and want to loaf. If these qualities are foremost in your character, you'll never make enough money to finance your own retirement anyway, so you'd better forget it unless you have some rich relatives somewhere.

No, what you want primarily is the freedom to pursue life as you choose. That's the blessing that retirement provides, this fourth phase of modern life. You cannot enjoy it to its full if you're going to be spending your days apprehensively reading the stock lists or worrying about next year's income or wondering if, after all, you did the right thing in quitting work so young.

If your emotional make-up won't allow you to blow the whistle on your career, sell out your holdings, and buy a reasonably safe portfolio of stocks *and then forget it,* retirement is not for you. You should work until you're forced to quit. There's no sense entering retirement with a feeling of foreboding, for it defeats the purpose of the whole effort.

However, if you went to the trouble and expense of buying this book, it seems likely that you *are* the type who can have a successful retirement career. Just remember, it takes just as much determination to be carefree and relaxed as it does to master any other career.

A successful retirement doesn't come just by wishing for it, any more than a successful practice "just comes" to a physician.

Chapter 17

Things to Do After Retirement

MY FATHER WOULD NEVER AGREE TO RETIRE, AND THERE ARE PROB-
ably thousands of men like him. The fact is, my father would
be a poor candidate for retirement, for his work dominated his
life, an intriguing, all-absorbing mistress. He found more pleasure in his work (which was running his own small manufac-
turing and distributing company) than ever he could find in
any more leisurely pursuit. He was the kind of fellow who, at
age sixty-five, embarked on an ambitious new financing program for his company.

There are some people, like my father, who never should
retire.

There are many others, however, who should begin to plan
for it early in life.

In a great many respects the compulsory retirement at age
sixty-five in many companies is a shame, for there is no such
thing as a wise young man and the wisdom of elders is needed
at a company's helm. Certainly a man, in these days, is not
"past his prime" when he reaches sixty-five. I know scores of
men well over sixty-five who have as much vigor as any youth,

more knowledge than any "well-seasoned" middle-aged veteran, *plus* wisdom which can be attained only with years.

Yet in the great averages which govern our country's economy, most people *want* to retire by sixty-five, or earlier, if possible. It is the purpose of this book to help them accomplish this retirement on their own initiative and, in so doing, to perhaps discourage the so-called "modern" penchant for demanding retirement security from our employers and from the government. This is about as "modern" a trend as the ancient Greek civilization, but that's a different story.

The fact is, retirement is good for our nation's economy.

We are entering a period where we're producing candidates for jobs faster than we're creating a need for jobs. This is the part of the Financial Revolution which, in history, is following the Industrial Revolution.

Our birth rate is doing nothing to help this situation. The increasing use of automation in our factories will, temporarily at least, cause some loss of jobs or, at best, some dislocations in the work force.

Thus, believe it or not, the average fellow who retires, now and in the several decades ahead will actually be doing the economy a good turn, if he remains self-sufficient. For in retirement he will remain a consumer and a spender, which means he'll be creating jobs for other people. Yet he'll have freed a job for someone else.

But many a man, like my dad, cannot contemplate the state of idleness without suffering the cold shudders. A person who has been active all his life cannot suddenly sit down and begin to rock on the front porch without undergoing some drastic personality changes.

It is necessary to have a sensible and practical retirement plan if only to keep from going mad from boredom. Moreover, many persons will want some activity which, without requiring too much time and effort, will produce some kind of income.

But it has to be a sensible plan.

How many times have you heard the city-bred fellow say, "I'd like to quit this job and *retire* to the country and buy a chicken farm." Or the farmer complain, "How I'd like to get away from the drudgery and move to the city so I could get an easy job in a factory."

Anyone with sense knows that running a chicken farm successfully is back-breaking work, and that working in a factory can be just as exhausting as nurse-maiding a herd of dairy cattle.

Yet if the city fellow had a retirement income, he could move to the country and raise a small flock of chickens to *supplement* his income.

Or the farmer, if he's mechanically inclined and if he possesses a retirement income of adequate size, might move to town and get some kind of part-time job in a small factory.

But it isn't *retiring* when you trade one tough career for another tough one.

It's possible, though, to swap a demanding career for a happy mixture of retirement and partial responsibility in some income-yielding field.

I know a city detective whose hobbies were boating and swordfishing. Each summer he'd take his two weeks' leave plus two weeks without pay so he could pursue his sport in the Block Island and Cape Cod waters where, once a year, the swordfish are taken.

When his retirement came he outfitted a fine blue-water boat and now, once a year, combines his hobby and favorite sport with a sensible income-yielding job, by going after swordfish as a business. The last report from him was that he had earned, beyond the cost of his boat, over $6000 in the latest season.

Another friend who had a love of salt water invested a small sum in a boat yard and now supervises activities from a comfortable chair near a hauling winch where he enjoys life to the full and earns a fair supplemental income. In wintertime when the yard is closed, he just takes it easy on the inland waterway aboard his small but adequate cruiser.

There's a man in north Georgia, the owner of a fine tourist court, who spent an enviable career in the life insurance industry in Hartford. He was a keen man with figures and a skiing fan of unparalleled enthusiasm. When he retired and then bought a tourist court in Georgia, I was amazed.

Seems he'd always wanted to own one and to run one.

He has the place running so efficiently it takes only a few hours of his time each day, but most important, he loves it.

Another friend who shoots golf in the low 70's has a splendid retirement job. He teaches novices who are too timid to approach the club professional. He does it by appointment so that his time is his own, as he wants it.

In an earlier chapter I mentioned the photographer who is now getting supplemental income by selling layouts to magazines.

As for myself, since I've been writing from the age of twelve, I have a built-in retirement job and one which, I trust, will do something to supplement my retirement income when the time comes.

It may not be necessary to line up a job to produce supplemental income when you retire. But it will certainly be necessary to line up something to do in the way of activity. You do not wish to spend the important fourth phase of your life playing gin rummy with idle companions; that is, unless you intend to play the game competitively with some definite goal in mind.

Develop a hobby, develop some interests, something you can take with you into retirement. At the very least, they'll provide you with much pleasure. And they might, if you're fortunate, provide you with some welcome revenue.

In my office as I work on this text are two thick manuscripts, both submitted by snow-haired men, who, in retirement, have become amateur economists. One thesis develops our need to return to the gold standard. The other, which I confess is too deep for me, has something to do with revising the measurements used in the Gross National Product. The point is, neither of these men is idle. Nor is either of them bored.

Chapter 18

Social Security Coverage

YOU CERTAINLY KNOW WHETHER OR NOT YOU'RE COVERED BY SOCIAL Security insurance. If you are, you're being taxed for it. You cannot choose whether you will or will not be covered. If you're included in the law, you're part of the Social Security plan.

Before you or your dependents can qualify for Social Security benefits you must have credit for a certain amount of work that was performed while you were insured by the SocSec. This is counted as "quarters of coverage" which may have been earned any time after 1936. A quarter of coverage is any calendar quarter of three months beginning January 1, April 1, July 1 or October 1 in which you are paid at least $50 in wages.

If you are self-employed and have net earnings of $400 or more in a year, you get credit for four quarters of coverage for that year, if you have paid your SocSec tax.

Should you wish to continue to work after age 65 you can count quarters of coverage acquired after that time if you need to in order to qualify as "fully insured." Once you have 40 quarters, (ten years) you will be fully insured for life.

You will receive Social Security benefits upon your retirement based upon your *average* earnings during your covered working life. To make things more complicated, this is not your *actual* earnings, but earnings evaluated on the Social Security maximum base.

For instance, if you were working in 1958, you and your employer paid Social Security taxes on income you received up to $4,800. Even if you earned $15,000 in 1958, you still can claim only $4,800 as your income for that year since that was the amount of your "insured income." If you earned only $3,500 that year, the $3,500 is all you can claim, for that is the amount on which you paid taxes.

To refresh your memory about those "maximum earnings bases:"

It was $3,600 in 1951, 1952, 1953 and 1954.

It was $4,200 in 1955, 1956, 1957 and 1958.

It was $4,800 in 1959, 1960, 1961, 1962, 1963, 1964 and 1965.

It was $6,600 in 1966 and 1967.

It was $7,800 in 1968, 1969, 1970 and 1971.

It was $9,000 in 1972.

It was $10,800 in 1973.

It was $12,000 in 1974 and thereafter.

If you will figure out your average earnings as they related to the SocSec maximum earnings base, you will be able to determine in the following table, how much you will receive in benefits when you retire at age 65. (To find your average, write down the maximum allowed you each year that you worked and divide by the number of years worked.)

Average Annual Earnings	Primary Retirement men or women, age 65	Dependent wife or husband, age 65	Husband and wife, age 65, combined
$ 1,000	91.00	45.50	136.50
2,000	141.60	70.80	212.40
3,000	174.80	87.40	262.20
4,000	205.80	102.90	308.70

5,000	238.60	119.30	357.90
6,000	269.70	134.90	404.60
7,000	302.20	151.10	453.30
8,000	335.30	167.70	503.00
9,000	354.50	177.30	531.80
10,000	371.50	185.80	557.30
11,000	388.50	194.30	582.80
12,000	404.50	202.30	606.80

Once every few years, at least once every four years, you should go to your local Federal Security Agency (address in your telephone book) and obtain Form OAR-7004, and mail the form to the Social Security Administration in Baltimore, Maryland, requesting a statement of wages credited to you.

Social Security will *help* you in retirement by providing you, at age sixty-five, with some supplementary income, provided you have been fully covered during your working years.

However, you should not plan your life so that you *depend* on Social Security in your old age. It isn't adequate to give you a decent retirement.

There are several other retirement systems, of course, in addition to those provided by company pensions. The Railroad Retirement Act, for instance, covers more than 1,500,000 workers with pensions averaging $67.50 monthly.

In addition there are the Civil Service Retirement systems covering thousands of government employees, including the military.

If Social Security or some such retirement benefit represents your only retirement income, you had better see that any heavy obligations are discharged before you "go on pension."

Chapter 19

The Formula for Independent Retirement

THERE IS NO MIRACULOUS METHOD ANYONE CAN APPLY AND BE absolutely assured of independence in retirement. You cannot lay down laws and say that if you do certain prescribed things, you will be guaranteed certain results. You cannot even set up patterns of behavior with certain rewards as in the Army, for instance, where a regular soldier knows that if he "keeps his nose clean" and obeys the regulations, he will gain, in the end, a virtually unimpeachable right to a pension.

There are, however, certain ground rules for the average career man and the self-employed which should, if followed, produce sufficient financial security to permit carefree retirement, and if they are observed soon enough in life and followed closely, they may, in some cases, permit retirement before the conventional retirement age.

When you're young:

Establish an ironclad *rule* for savings. Save regularly and consistently.

Buy as much life insurance as you can afford.

Periodically convert some of your savings to the purchase of good common stocks.

Buy your own home if possible, so that you may "save" while paying rent to yourself in the form of a mortgage.

Through your middle years:

Continue to save as regularly and as consistently as ever.

Continue to convert regularly some of your savings into securities.

Buy more life insurance whenever you feel you can afford it.

If you have the money, you can start buying your retirement home, though this is not necessary at this time.

Be developing some hobbies, some outside interests that you'd like to pursue in greater depth when you have more leisure.

Start "shopping around" for the place you'd like to live in once you've retired.

One year before you retire:

Make a complete appraisal of all your assets including savings, cash-surrender value of your insurance policies, total value of your investment portfolio, equity in your real estate (based on resale value).

Pay off any long-term obligations.

Avoid contracting for new obligations.

If there are young children under twenty-two, earmark funds in savings bonds, a savings account, paid-up insurance, or other investments to finance their education and "give them a start."

When you retire:

Cash in most of your life insurance policies.

Set aside a paid-up life insurance policy for final expenses.

Set aside some paid-up life insurance policies, if you wish, for other beneficiaries to whom you wish to make bequests. This would include your children or other relatives.

If you live in a large home, and your children are all grown, put it up for sale and move to a small, paid-for home.

Withdraw your surplus savings from your savings account, leaving a sum for emergencies.

With cash from your insurance policies, your surplus savings, your sale of the house and sale of "speculative" stocks in your portfolio, create a new, safe portfolio of investments.

Check your will. Make sure it provides what you wish.

Have a good physical checkup for yourself and your wife, both medical and dental.

Send Form OAR-7004 to the Social Security Administration, Baltimore, Maryland, to make sure you'll be credited with the proper Social Security retirement benefits when the time comes. (See Chapter 18.)

Set up a rigid new budget based on your expected retirement income, leaving, if possible, some leeway in case your dividend yield isn't as high as expected.

After you've retired:

At first just do what you want, to help you cushion the transition from work to retirement. If you've always wanted to drive your car from coast to coast, drive; if you've always wanted to cruise the inland waterway, cruise; if you've always wanted to just sit in the sun and think, sit and think.

Allow yourself at least six months to become adjusted to retirement. Experience shows that active people require at least that much time to get in the "retirement frame of mind."

Later pursue your hobbies or your special interests, the hobbies and interests you should have been developing since middle life or earlier.

Above all, enjoy yourself!

Chapter 20

Life's Fourth Phase

SOME PEOPLE LOVE OLIVES THE FIRST TIME THEY EAT THEM. OTHERS
have to learn to like them. Anyone who likes them, though,
whether the taste was spontaneous or acquired, says they're
one of God's finer fruits. So it is with retirement. Some take to
it with gusto. Some have to learn to like it. No initiate would
ever give it up.

Retirement, now possible to nearly everyone, is life's fourth
phase, following in order, the childhood years, the educational
years, and the productive years. It is a reward; it is virtually a
right.

Nothing is more misdirected than the life of a man who feels
he must keep working "until the end" to accumulate more and
more possessions for his heirs and survivors. For what? So the
heirs can take it easy and reap the reward the beavering
worker should have had?

Yet this reward, this fourth phase, sometimes comes hard to
some folks. They have good reason, for retirement is likely to
come as a mental and emotional shock. It's an important step,
like the first day of school, like landing the first job, or like

getting married. Like marriage, it's nearly an irrevocable step. It's a plunge into the unknown.

You approach it with mixed feelings. There's considerable regret, for it marks a milestone and terminates a phase of life like graduation day from college. There's anxiety and apprehension. There's the anticipated freedom and relief from responsibility. There's the glimmering idea that you've won the battle and are now about to become king of your own domain.

One minute you think of the fun you're going to have with your spare time. The next, you hold back tears as you protest, "But I can't give all this up."

Then the Big Day comes and you get your gold watch or your outboard motor from your colleagues, you make your speech, you shake all the hands, and you celebrate and reiterate the corny jokes.

And you go home and to bed.

The next day is the hollowest day of your life. You are lost. You are torn between depression and wild, near-hysterical laughter, like coming out of gas in the dentist's chair, or the first day after giving up smoking.

Have you ever noticed a wild creature when it's freed from a cage, a canary, a white mouse, a rabbit, a parakeet, a squirrel? First it pokes its head tentatively out the door, then it gingerly samples the outside with one foot. Even when it's completely out of the cage, it looks around, confused and bewildered, before making the dash to freedom.

Instinct makes a wild thing seize the opportunity and *run* or *fly* to freedom as soon as the confusion of civilized confinement is overcome. With humans there is no instinct, for it has been suppressed for centuries. We must *learn* to enjoy freedom.

This is the business of getting adjusted.

First you must realize that you're not on the shelf. You are not being retired so you can make way for a younger man; you are being retired as a reward for your labors.

You must not step aside, for you have a priceless possession, wisdom. I have said earlier in this treatise, but it bears repeating: *There is no such thing as a wise young man.* In your retirement share your wisdom, the gift of years, with those who possess only knowledge and intelligence because they have not lived long enough to have wisdom.

About the first impression a retired man has is an awakened appreciation of his wife. After hanging around the house a few days, a man soon comes to the conclusion that about the most efficient person he has ever encountered is his wife, for he'll marvel at the amount of work and organizational ability required to run a home effectively.

It's not uncommon for a man, in this early period of retirement, to assert his masculinity by seizing hammer and nails, paint and brush, screw driver and awl, and go about repairing and restoring those things which have always been a mystery to his wife.

Nevertheless, care should be taken not to let household chores become the major occupation in your life.

You have hobbies and outside interests, remember?

Looking back, you'll recall that it wasn't, after all, so hard to complete the high school courses or college courses that prepared you for your career.

Well, it's no harder to complete the adjustment that will prepare you for life's golden fourth phase.

The only difference is, you have no instructors and no instructions.

It's something you'll have to work out yourself.

But the reward is worth it.

Chapter 21

A Classical Plan

WHEN YOU'RE READY TO RETIRE YOU MAY LIKELY HAVE ACCUMULATED enough in savings and in a pension fund to afford you a life of carefree living for the rest of your days.

If so, you're fortunate.

There are many, however, who will not have such a well-set-up program. Yet those persons without a company pension or without annuities can probably stop work at retirement age *if they have managed their lives properly.*

The first step is to tote up your assets.

How big is your savings account?

How much cash-surrender value do you possess in insurance?

How much equity do you own in your home?

How much is your portfolio of securities worth?

What other assets do you own?

How much can you expect from Social Security?

Perhaps you can sell your home and buy a smaller, less expensive one. Perhaps you'll want to live where the climate is milder and your fuel and clothes bills won't be so high. Certainly you won't want to carry so much life insurance.

Consider these—and other angles that might occur to you—and then count up your assets again.

In all likelihood, you'll find out that you can really *afford* to retire.

And this, in fact, is the secret of retirement, of being able to retire.

A great many people do not start planning for it while they are young enough to control their destinies.

Many more never seem to realize how wealthy they really are, for they never take time to count up their assets.

If you save while you're young—with cash, bonds, insurance, a home, and real estate,

And if you continue to save *some* of your money and invest *some* of your savings during your middle years,

You should be able to retire on your combined savings and investments without undue worry.

This is not a formula. It is simple organization of a breadwinner's productive years. There is no magic, and it is certainly no panacea, for many times the going will be rough, particularly when it comes to saving.

But it's possible to do.

You owe it to yourself to try it.

Glossary of Stock Market Terms
You Should Know

THE PURPOSE OF THIS BOOK IS NOT TO TELL YOU WHAT TO DO IN retirement but to tell you how to save your money and how to invest your money so that you may enjoy a secure retirement. It is based on the principle of saving plus investing to help you accumulate the necessary funds for retirement.

When you first become an investor there are numerous terms that may sound strange to you.

Here is a glossary of some of the most common terms and expressions used on Wall Street:

Accrued dividends. In the case of cumulative preferred stock, where dividends must be paid before dividends can be paid on common stock, if the dividends are past due but have not been paid, they are said to be accrued dividends.

Accumulation. The unpublicized purchase of large quantities of a particular security, usually done before the market rises in that particular stock.

Allotment. When a new offering of securities is made, an investment banking firm or syndicate makes an allotment to a purchaser prior to the offering.

Amortization. Installment payments on a long-term debt, or, in the case of bonds, the gradual writing off of a premium paid for a bond selling above par at the time of purchase.

Arbitrage. Applied usually in terms of foreign currencies when a person buys in one market and sells in another in order to take advantage of a disparity in price.

Arrears. An unpaid debt, overdue.

Assets, net. A company's net depreciated assets, minus all its liabilities other than to stockholders.

Assets, total. A corporation's total value, what it owns, plus all the money owed to it. Assets may be tangible or intangible. They may be fixed, current, or deferred.

At the market. A term used in authorizing a broker to buy a security in your name at the "going price."

Balance sheet. A summary showing in one column a corporation's principal assets, and in a corresponding column, its liabilities.

Bear. A stock trader who expects that some securities or commodities will decrease in price. He expects to buy them at a lower price in the future and may sell short in anticipation of the price drop.

Bear market. So described when the influence of bears (above) is predominant and the price trend is lower.

Bear raid. Heavy selling of a security to depress the price suddenly.

Bid and asked. Respective prices at which a buyer will purchase and a seller will sell.

Bid and asked list (in newspapers). The bid and asked prices of stocks which were not traded in the previous session of the stock market, hence whose quotes do not appear in the regular list of quotations.

Big Board. The New York Stock Exchange.

Blue sky laws. Regulations in the various states governing the purchase, sale, and issuance of securities.

Board lot. Same as round lot: the unit of trade on the New York Stock Exchange—100 shares of security or $1000 par value of a bond.

Bond. A note which says that the owner of the bond has

loaned money to the issuer of the bond and that the issuer promises to pay interest and to repay the loan on a specified date.

Bond, debenture. A bond not secured by any specific claim on the property of the issuer, backed by the credit standing of the company.

Bond, mortgage. A bond guaranteed by a specific lien on a specific piece of the company's property.

Bonds, bonus. Bonds issued to promoters of a project or development as a reward for their services, usually in lieu of cash. Bonus bonds are also issued by some states and municipalities to induce manufacturers to locate in their state or town.

Bonus stock. Stock issued to purchasers when a new issue is brought out; usually common stock issued to purchasers of preferred shares.

Book. A memorandum book in which a stock-exchange specialist keeps tab of his buying and selling orders which have yet to be executed.

Boon. A rapid or steady rise in prices in the stock market, or a pronounced advance in business.

Brokers' loans. Loans made to brokers by banks with securities used as collateral, representing the money needed to carry the floating supply of speculative, or very active, securities.

Bucket shop. A shady brokerage firm. A dishonest broker.

Bull. A trader who expects a rise in the prices of securities and commodities and who has bought stocks and commodities in anticipation.

Bull market. A market with sudden or sustained rises in prices.

Call. A contract which entitles its holder to buy specified securities or commodities at a fixed price within a specified period of time. The opposite of a "Put."

Callable bonds. Bonds which may be redeemed by the company before the maturity date.

Capital. The amount an individual or a corporation has to invest or has already invested.

Capital (accounting term). The excess of assets over liabilities, or "net worth."

Capitalization. The total of the authorized par value of stocks and bonds of a corporation, added to surplus.

Cash grain, or *spot grain.* Grain available for immediate delivery.

Common stock. A corporation's "junior" security, which receives no protection in case of failure until all prior obligations have been discharged. It represents ownership of an equity in the business, but only after all other claims have been met.

Coupon bonds. Bonds not issued to a particular person but which have coupons attached which may be clipped and redeemed for specified amounts of interest.

Customers' men. Employees of brokerage houses who solicit business or handle customers' accounts or who advise the customers about the buying or selling of securities.

Discretionary orders. Orders to a broker to buy or sell securities on his own judgment, at the risk of the customer.

Diversification. A combination of investments in portfolio, accomplished by acquiring the securities and bonds of different companies in different industries at different dates.

Dividend, cash. The payment made to stockholders.

Dividend, stock. The issuance of stock by the company to registered stockholders in lieu of or in addition to cash dividends.

Dow theory. A theory developed by the late William Peter Hamilton, former editor of the *Wall Street Journal,* for predicting stock market trends. It uses the chart action of averages of prices of rail stocks and industrial stocks to determine whether the market is bullish or bearish.

Earnings per share. The amount of profit made by a company after taxes and deductions for all prior charges and depreciation, divided by the number of shares of stock it has outstanding. This has no bearing on whether or not dividends have been paid out.

Ex-dividend. When a dividend is declared, a date is set for taking a record of stockholders entitled to receive it. After this date the stock is quoted without the dividend and it is said to have gone "ex-dividend."

Fiscal year. The accounting year as distinguished from the calendar year.

Fluctuation. Variation in price.

Free ride. By purchasing securities at their original subscription price and selling them within a few hours after they are first offered to the public at a higher price than you paid for them, you are said to have had a free ride. The term comes from earlier days when stocks did not have to be paid for until they were delivered; and it applies today even though you must pay for your securities in advance.

Frozen assets. Assets of a corporation which are not readily convertible to cash.

Futures. Contracts in commodities whereby the seller promises to deliver a specific quantity of the commodity at a future date. There is active trading in "futures contracts" in many commodities.

Gilt-edged. The highest quality securities available.

Hypothecate. To deposit securities (sometimes other collateral) as a pledge for the repayment of a loan.

Inactive post. The name of a post on the floor of the New York Stock Exchange where relatively inactive securities are traded in round lots of 10 shares. Full lots are 100 shares at other posts.

Income account. Summary of a company's revenue, expenses, and profits or losses for a specific period.

Interest. Payments to you for use of your money.

Interest, compound. Interest paid upon previously accumulated interest.

Interim dividend. A small dividend paid during the year in anticipation of a final dividend at the end of the fiscal year.

Investment. To put a sum of money to work for you in a place where it can be expected to earn an income or some kind of annual return. When used in Wall Street it sometimes means the opposite of "speculation." Hence it means capital put into an enterprise for a long period to yield a moderate return with greatest safety.

Issue. A bond, stock, or other obligation.

Lamb. An inexperienced purchaser of securities, prone to speculate.

Legal bonds. Bonds of the highest rating, accepted by states and the federal government for investments.

Leverage. The effect on earnings of a corporation of its borrowed money. It may permit greater profits to stockholders. Also it is the power of advantage or disadvantage said to accrue to the securities in a mutual fund in a rising or declining market.

Liquid assets. Assets which can be converted immediately to cash. They may also be called current assets in an industrial firm.

Liquidation. The end of a business and sale of all its possessions.

Liquidity. The percentage of assets that may be converted to cash.

Loan crowd (Loan boys). The group of brokers on the floor of the New York Stock Exchange who borrow and lend stock for "shorts."

Long. When you "go long" (i.e., the opposite of "short") you hold securities or commodities in anticipation of a price rise.

Margin. The amount of money you deposit with your broker for the purchase of stocks or commodities, the balance to be paid later. The amount of margin you must pay is determined by regulation of the Federal Reserve Board.

Margin account. An arrangement by which you borrow from a broker to buy more shares of a security than you really pay for in cash. The account operates somewhat like a line of credit in a bank.

Melon. A large stock or cash dividend.

Odd lot. An amount of stock which is less than the required unit of trading, such as less than the 100-share "lot" on the New York Stock Exchange or American Stock Exchange.

Odd-lot dealers. Members of the New York Stock Exchange who specialize in odd lots, handling them for regular commission brokers. They charge a small differential for the service.

Out-of-line. Securities selling either too high or too low, usually the former.

Over-the-counter market. The trading of securities not listed on the New York Stock Exchange or the American Stock Exchange or on any one of the regional exchanges. Bid and asked prices are obtained by brokers and these are communicated by the National Association of Securities Dealers.

Paper. Short-term evidences of indebtedness.

Par. The asserted "value" of stock per share, declared by a company upon original issuance. The amount is engraved on the face of the stock. The term is more important when applied to bonds as it indicates the value originally received in the issuing corporation and the amount due to the investor at maturity.

Parity, commodities. The equalization of two delivery points.

Parity, farm. A predetermined price for farm commodities which is said to yield the farmer in income the same standard of living as the industrial worker.

Parity, foreign exchange. The value of one currency in terms of another, determined by their respective gold backing.

Participating bonds. Bonds which not only receive a stated rate of interest but also share in excess profits of the issuing corporation.

Peg. To keep the market for anything within a stated range.

Plunger. Reckless speculator.

Pool. A group of persons, usually a combination of several kinds of expert, organized to exploit the market in certain stock or stocks. Members usually agree not to trade separately for their own accounts.

Portfolio. The total of an investor's capital which is committed to stocks and bonds or other securities of a long-range nature.

Profit-taking (Profit-cashing). Selling securities in order to realize the cash profit.

Prospectus. A printed document detailing the organization of a new business or the expansion plans of an existing company.

Proxy. Written authority given by a stockholder to someone else permitting the second party to vote the stock at a stockholders' meeting.

Put. An option to sell an amount of stock to the writer of the option at a specified price within a period of time agreed upon.

Pyramiding. Using paper profits as the basis for more margin credit with which to buy more securities.

Quick assets. Like liquid assets, readily salable.

Raid. Usually spontaneous. Active buying or selling to shake out weakly margined traders. A bear raid would mean heavy selling to cause small traders to liquidate. A bull raid would force shorts to cover.

Rally. A spirited upturn in the market, usually of short duration.

Reaction. The ending and reversal of any trend in the market or in any particular stock.

Rigging. Manipulation.

Rights. These are specified privileges granted to stockholders, permitting them to buy a new stock or bond at a price below the prevailing market.

Share. Means the same as stock. Or, it determines the unit of stock, as one share of stock, two shares of stock, etc.

Short covering. The buying back by a trader who has sold stocks he did not own.

Short sale. The sale of stocks or commodities which are not owned, in anticipation of being able to buy them back later at a lower price. In dealing thus with securities the seller must borrow the securities with which to make delivery. In commodities, the seller promises to make delivery at some future date.

Specialist. A member of the stock exchange who acts as a "broker's broker," keeping a record of the selling and buying orders of other exchange members in certain specified stocks. He keeps a book on all transactions, including a G.T.C. list (orders which are "good till countermanded").

Speculation. Putting capital into an enterprise for quick and large returns at a greater-than-normal risk.

Spot. Commodities which can be delivered readily.

Spread. The difference between the bid and asked price of a security.

Stop order. An order given to a broker to protect a profit or limit a loss.

Straddle. A combination of puts and calls on the same security.

Under-the-rule. If a member of the exchange does not deliver a security in accordance with terms of a contract, an official of the exchange will buy the security and make delivery, bringing the broker "under the rule."

Unlisted securities. Securities not registered or listed on an organized exchange. Usually traded over the counter.

Watered stock. One of the least understood and most misused terms. It is stock of a corporation issued to members of the corporation and other "insiders" for a nominal consideration and without a fair increase in the assets of the corporation. Thus it dilutes the value behind each share held by the investors. Under no circumstances does it mean a widely distributed stock, just because it is widely owned. Nor does it mean a stock which has been split in price.